T0273652

Loving What's Next

Praise for *Loving What's Next*

I personally know Michelle Barr and love her new book, *Loving What's Next: What You Want Can Be Yours Now!* It's a roadmap to helping women through challenging life transitions and into what they truly desire. A tonic for troubling times. Read it.

-Dr. Joe Vitale, #1 best-selling author of
Zero Limits and *The Miracle*

I know Michelle personally, and what a powerhouse she is. I've seen her take action on intuitive 'hits' without hesitation, creating miracles and magic time and time again. She is truly a master and inspiration. Because of that, I'm confident that *Loving What's Next: What You Want Can Be Yours Now!* can and will change the trajectory of your life if you follow her plan. I highly recommend it!

-Lisa Winston, #1 best-selling author,
inspirational speaker, and artist

If anyone knows how to create positive change and manifest BIG desires quickly, it's Michelle Barr. In a world of smoke and mirrors, Michelle is a rare gem of an experienced mentor who walks her talk. Through her wisdom, practices, and genuine love revealed in *Loving What's Next*, you will discover your power and step into your highest potential of what's next for you.

-Gina DeVee, author of *The Audacity to be Queen*

Dr. Michelle Barr's *Loving What's Next* is an essential read for those ready to level-up and make their dreams a reality! This comprehensive workbook provides the keys to unlock your inner potential and manifest what you desire. With her extensive expertise and personal wisdom, she empowers you to clear the obstacles and create the life of your dreams. Prepare to be inspired, empowered, and ready to embrace your next adventure!

-**Maurielle Lue,** Fox News Anchor and TV Personality

Loving What's Next is a roadmap for people navigating life's transitions and on the verge of a breakthrough. Dr. Michelle Barr provides the guidance and support you are seeking to achieve your deepest desires and create a life you love living. In her book, she shares her expertise, experience, and wisdom to help you transform yourself and your world from where you are to where you want to be. What a gift to see Dr. Michelle's gifts in action and available to all here!

-**Danelle Delgado,** International Speaker and Business Strategist, Media Personality, and author of *I Choose Joy: The Daily Gratitude Practice That Will Transform Your Life*

Loving What's Next is a road map unlocking life's secrets for you to follow. It has been carefully laid out step by step. Just open the book and start to see your life magically shift. Be prepared to be amazed when you discover the truth in "What you want can be yours."

-**Maria Verdeschi,** #1 best-selling author of *There Is No Death, Only Life*

Every chapter is a question that will make you dig deeper into the curiosities of who you really are and what it is you truly seek. As a former coaching client, I can vow that Michelle is a mirror for helping you to see your truest potential.

-**Margo Reilly,** empowerment mentor, speaker, and author of
When the Apple Falls Far From the Tree

What truly sets *Loving What's Next* apart is its practicality. It doesn't just inspire; it equips. It doesn't just encourage; it empowers. It provides the tools and strategies to handle whatever obstacles life may throw in your path, ensuring that nothing derails your journey to what you desire. A transformative lifeline, guiding women through change. Practical steps to align desires, heal, and embrace the future with confidence.

-**Becc Nelson,** LMFT licensed therapist and
spiritual coach, best-selling author of
Cut the Shit: Reframe Your Thinking, Regain Your Life

Michelle Barr beautifully weaves together the art of coaching, personal anecdotes, and profound wisdom to create a comprehensive guide that addresses the heart and soul of women seeking transformation. Her nurturing guidance will help you not only weather the storms of transition but also thrive as you embrace the power of change.

-**Jill M. Jackson**, spiritual teacher, retreat leader, and author of
Mississippi Medium and Children of the New Earth

Michelle Barr is a master at helping you shift your thoughts to move you forward on your life journey so you can truly receive everything you want and desire. She is a brilliant coach and spiritual advisor. If you are looking to live your best and most fulfilling life, *Loving What's Next* is a must read!

-Joan Frank, President, B Frank Communications

Loving What's Next

What You Want Can Be Yours Now!

Dr. Michelle Barr

NEW YORK

LONDON • NASHVILLE • MELBOURNE • VANCOUVER

Loving What's Next

What You Want Can Be Yours Now!

© 2025 Dr. Michelle Barr

All rights reserved. No portion of this book may be reproduced, stored in a retrieval system, or transmitted in any form or by any means—electronic, mechanical, photocopy, recording, scanning, or other—except for brief quotations in critical reviews or articles, without the prior written permission of the publisher.

Published in New York, New York, by Morgan James Publishing. Morgan James is a trademark of Morgan James, LLC. www.MorganJamesPublishing.com

Proudly distributed by Publishers Group West®

Morgan James BOGO™

A **FREE** ebook edition is available for you or a friend with the purchase of this print book.

CLEARLY SIGN YOUR NAME ABOVE

Instructions to claim your free ebook edition:
1. Visit MorganJamesBOGO.com
2. Sign your name CLEARLY in the space above
3. Complete the form and submit a photo of this entire page
4. You or your friend can download the ebook to your preferred device

ISBN 9781636984155 paperback
ISBN 9781636984162 ebook
Library of Congress Control Number: 2023952576

Cover Design by:
Rachel Lopez
www.r2cdesign.com

Morgan James PUBLISHING

Builds

with...

Habitat for Humanity® Peninsula and Greater Williamsburg

Morgan James is a proud partner of Habitat for Humanity Peninsula and Greater Williamsburg. Partners in building since 2006.

Get involved today! Visit: www.morgan-james-publishing.com/giving-back

Midlife is when the Universe gently places her hands upon your shoulders, pulls you close, and whispers in your ear: I'm not screwing around. All of this pretending and performing—these coping mechanisms that you've developed to protect yourself from getting hurt—has to go. Your armor is preventing you from growing into your gifts. I understand that you needed these protections when you were small. I understand that you believed your armor could help you secure all of the things you needed to feel worthy and lovable, but you're still searching and you're more lost than ever. Time is growing short. There are unexplored adventures ahead of you. You can't live the rest of your life worried about what other people think. You were born worthy of love and belonging. Courage and daring are coursing through your veins. You were made to live and love with your whole heart. It's time to show up and be seen.

—Brené Brown

Contents

Acknowledgments

Through all the ages and seasons, I am blessed with loving and unconditional support, even when it sounds crazy or it doesn't look yet like it's going to work out.

My husband, Roger, you have lived with me since before this whole way of living and being started, stuck by me when it was all a chaotic mess, and cheered me on, supporting me every step of the way as I built this thing for me and for us. I appreciate you immensely and love you dearly. Look what we've created! I am excited for What's Next.

Craig, Hannah, and Haley, the magnificent beings who are my children, you have been on this journey with me since you arrived here on this planet and in my life, and I treasure you. As I heal and grow and evolve, you do, also. I am excited to watch you creating lives you love and to be able to support you and cheer you on! I am excited for What's Next.

Spiritual running buddies, friends, family, and colleagues, I could not have gotten here without you! You each had a part in who I am today, and I appreciate all the love and support you have always given me and continue to provide in this journey we are all on together. A reason, a season, or a lifetime, you all matter. Thank you for all the adventures we have shared. I am excited for What's Next.

My beloved spiritual teachers, coaches, mentors, and thought leaders who have been with me from the beginning or stepped in anywhere along the way to help me through the growing pains, the uplevels, the quantum leaps, to push me to continue this Hero's Journey, ever following my desires and clearing, healing, and resolving what was in my way, I am so grateful for you in my life, and I think about you often. I hear your words in my head. It helps me keep going to What's Next.

To my nine-year-old self, you did it! Here's your NY Book Publishing deal.

What's Next?

Preface: A Letter to the Reader

To You, the Reader,

People call me and email me every day telling me what they most want and why they don't and can't have it.

Too many people never take any action toward what they say they want most then wonder why they don't have it. This leads to one of two things: a lot of shame, blame, guilt, self-doubt, self-sabotage, and anger turned inward; or resentment, criticism, judgment, shame, blame, and anger turned outward toward those who have created what they want to be, do, and have, or toward those you perceive are in your way.

The Truth is, you are what's in your way. Period. I will always tell you the truth, even when it's hard to hear, especially when it's hard to hear.

I spent a lot of years not having what I said I wanted most, and I had a lot of reasons why I didn't have it, couldn't have it, shouldn't have it, or just not now. Then, I made a decision to have it, right now. I took Action. I didn't just start running around doing, doing, doing, though. I cleared the mental and emotional clutter. I made a decision, I owned it 100 percent, I created a vision of the life I wanted to live, and I took inspired aligned action.

Now, I have the life I want to live and everything that supports and sustains it. I have the business I love that allows me to serve in my purpose, this fully integrated life doing only what I am made to do rather than just what I can do. I have healed relationships and money in the bank, because I have healed my relationship with money, too.

I believe this journey, the Hero's Journey, is an intensive one. It will grow you like nothing else. At this point in my Journey, I would never go back. The payoffs are so worth it. There are just some things you are going to want to know, so I wrote them down for you here.

To me, this is the ultimate Freedom—money freedom, yes; time freedom, yes, this has come in over the past few years once I mastered money freedom; and most importantly, the freedom to have the Journey I came here for without money, time, resources, and others making these most important decisions for me. I see so many people doing the opposite. They are living a life dictated by the work they are doing and the conditions created by it, and they are living their life based on what they have right now, and by the wants, needs, desires, and expectations of others. They don't love what they are doing, and they don't even like their lives. Year after year, nothing changes. Year after year, they keep telling themselves they are going to have what they most want and live the life they most want to live . . . someday.

If you are ready to be committed to living the life that you most want to live, I want you to know you can live that life now and at every season and stage. What you want CAN be yours NOW!

It's so possible and more doable than you believe it is. So, borrow the belief I have in you until you can believe in yourself. People hire me every day to help them do what I have done and what I know how to support and guide you in doing. I have been where you are. I have lived it over and over again. For way too long.

Then the day came when I stopped talking about not having it and decided to have it instead.

Once you discover how to give yourself this Freedom, you will be able to do it every time you find yourself in a place where you identify that there is something you most want that you don't have.

This book is not for people who want to stay in lives they don't love doing work they don't like, surrounded by people and things that no longer serve them. What I am going to share with you is for people who are ready to make a decision to get clear on what they most want and then take action to create it for themselves.

I am asking you right here to Trust the Process.

The principles I share with you in this book are things I apply to living my life in all areas and to building and growing my business, as well.

Maybe you aren't feeling very creative, intuitive, or inspired right now? That's okay. This work will open you up to accessing more of yourself and bringing it out into the world.

This book and these principles will be especially embraced by life coaches, business coaches, counselors, teachers, speakers, authors, helpers, and healers of all kinds. I know this, because I have a proven track record of working with them.

These same clients and students I have served, along with others in my community, are just like you, looking to create some midlife magic, wanting to take their power back and manifest a new and better life for this age and season, go deeper into their true selves and rediscover who they are and what is there; desiring to retire earlier than planned and to be able to create a way to do that, wanting to have more money when they decid to retire, hoping it's not too late to begin an encore career or a heart-based project that means so much to them, or reinventing themselves and their lives after a divorce or other life-altering transition.

We will start here.

Create A Vision. => M.O.V.E. => Create A Life.

Love and Fire,
Michelle

Introduction

This book is coming to you after thirty-three years of recon-
structing, changing, and upleveling my life, of learning
how to create a life I love and then live it full out. Over and
over again. I have grown and transformed, and, along this magnificent journey, I have learned how to engage with the process and
become the conscious creator of my own life. I have also learned
very well that WHAT YOU WANT CAN BE YOURS NOW and
how to teach this to you.

This is about getting so focused, clear, grounded, and centered
into who you are and what you Desire, and then allowing yourself
to embody it more fully so that it shows up in your outer world.
At first, it will be things you are learning to do, tools, techniques,
principles, processes, and practices, and, if you stay with it, it can
become a way of living and being that unfolds your life before you
with much more ease and grace and swiftness. This is my journey,
and I had to perfect it before teaching it to you.

A big part of creating my life has been through the path of creating my own purpose-led business that supports and sustains the

1

life I want to live, and giving myself the freedom to pursue heart-based projects. As you read this, you may realize you have these same desires, and you will find support and guidance here. You may be searching for something else, and this breadcrumb showed up (more on that later). An Encore Career. A more aligned and lucrative way to spend your years after retirement. Creating more money for retirement. Or, a more fulfilling way to achieve success and receive income than what you have now.

During our time together, I will ask you as I ask all my clients and students, to make a commitment to yourself to see this through. I am going to help you discover and decide what you really, really want, and, just as importantly, to learn to let go of what no longer serves you. This part is even more crucial than you may think, and I am going to tell you why as well as how.

Then, we will move into the plan. One of the things I am recognized for is taking inspired action and teaching others how to understand and take aligned inspired action. I have learned from the masters, and I have applied this to my own life for decades. It is key.

One tool I have, you can start using right now. Begin Day One of my twenty-one-day free email course, "How to Move Forward In Any Area of Your Life," by signing up at www.IntuitiveSuccessCoach.com.

And, I will help you with my true expertise, how to handle what comes up when you start moving toward your dreams and desires. We are going to identify and eradicate self-sabotage that is running your show and driving your bus, most often unconsciously. We will clean up the stuff that is getting in your way and keeping you from moving forward. I will lead you through making peace with your past to gain power for your future. You will discover how to transform core issues to thrive and shift your relationship with money. By the end of our time together, you will be so much more connected with your "What's Next." Not only will you have started creating it, but you will have started seeing the results show up in your life and your world.

Freedom is one of my highest core values. Another is to help you #FindYourFreedom. You will see as I share my journey with you, that, at first, I desired to have more freedom to be who I was and to do what I am made to do. Along the way, I desired money freedom, and I created that. A mentor once taught me, true financial freedom is not how much money you have in the bank; true financial freedom is knowing how to create and receive all the money you want and need when you want and need it. Powerful turning point for me! In more recent years, with us retiring my husband from his lifetime career in education, and my first and then second grandbabies showing up, I began to recognize a deep desire for Time Freedom that had not really been there before. I love what I do. I have created a life where I do now what I am made to do and here to do, not just things I can do. And, I have an entrepreneurial spirit. So, I already combine and integrate work and play and my life a lot. Suddenly, I wanted more and different levels of time freedom. It is what I set out to create for myself and my family, and I did it using what I am teaching you and guiding you through in this book.

Do not worry. There are things inside of you that will guide your way. Even when my clients are stuck in the utmost state of confusion, I lead them back to their desires. I always trust their desires. I know that, where there is a desire, a way has already been made. I have come to trust this 100 percent.

Holding this book in my hand illustrates my point. When I was just nine years old, I picked up a pencil and notepad and started writing a book. Not just that, though. I began telling my parents that I needed to send my book out to Publishers, because I was going to have a New York Publisher. I went to the library and got a copy of the *Writer's Digest*, and I looked up publishers and sent them my manuscripts. They wrote me back—my first rejection letters. In my early twenties, I wrote a novel, and I got an Agent who took my book to New York City to pitch it to Publishers there. I got so close. Then life took many turns for me, and I got busy doing life, as we tend to do. Until, I learned how to take control and responsibility for all of my life and create the life and the results I needed, wanted, and desired. That journey has now become this book. With so much grace and ease and swiftness, a New York Publisher offered me a book deal. And, here we are.

I got here by connecting with my truest desires, following the breadcrumbs, taking aligned, inspired action, and cleaning up all that came up to derail me along the way. I did all the things I am now going to teach you so that your truest desires can be made manifest in your life.

I still remember the day over a decade ago, sitting in San Diego in a conference aimed at getting me in touch with and connected to my big mission and my big life, and the woman on stage looking right at me, asked, "Are you merely interested or committed?"

Wow! What a question. That one not only spoke to me; it reached out and grabbed me by the shoulders and shook me a little. Up until that moment, I had been dabbling, playing in the possibilities, dreaming about all the things I could do and would do. I had big intentions. And yet, I was dancing around the edges, dipping my toe in, surveying the surface, without diving in.

She called me to action that day, and nothing has ever been the same since. Everything I had learned and experienced up to that moment had prepared me to step into the fullness of it. All I had to do was show up, just as I was.

You have everything inside of you in this moment that you need.

I am calling you to action.

Sound great? Let's get M.O.V.E.'ing!

PART ONE

Decide What You Want

CHAPTER 1

Are You Receiving Data or Inspiration?

T he highest state of being to create from is when you are able to be where you are here and now and find the appreciation in that, and, at the same time, to connect with and step into where you want to go and who you want to be in your future. The key is to maintain both of these states simultaneously and to love them. Thus, the title of this book—*Loving What's Next.*

It takes a lot of energy to create what you desire, and for most people this means clearing and cleaning the mental and emotional clutter that is jamming up your channels. This not only takes its toll on you mentally and emotionally, but it settles into the physical and starts creating all kinds of dis-ease.

We receive information in only two ways; data and inspiration. Data comes from the mind. We are going to talk a lot about the mind and the changes you are going to need to make in how you think about and work with your mind. When we are seeking solutions to our problems, the mind wants to be oh so helpful, and it gets to work. The issue is that the mind operates like a computer. It can only go back through your database and bring you information based on what was before. Not only that, but the mind is heavily weighted to keep you safe and alive, not necessarily to support you to grow and thrive. The mind lies to you. It is affected by your programming and conditioning, much of which was embedded and anchored into you by the age of seven.

You have a Higher Self, a Higher Mind, and it is directly connected to the Divine Intelligence in whatever way you conceive of this. This is who you are, who you were before all the programming and conditioning, and who you came here to be. When you are able to access this part of you, to trust it, to allow it to lead, and to learn to connect with the Source that created it, you will move from areas where you are merely surviving to thriving. You can do this in any and all areas of your life. Great news! Think of this as an interconnected web. All that you do in one area directly affects all areas. It changes you from the inside out and has a powerful impact on your life and your world.

Look all around you. Nature is always moving toward more life. Nothing in nature stops short of its fullest potential as long as it is alive. That is within us, too.

The more you clear the mental and emotional clutter, the more open you are to receiving inspiration, which is new and now, and pointing you in the direction of receiving and achieving your desires.

Einstein said, "The intuitive mind is a sacred gift and the rational mind is a faithful servant. We have created a society that honors the servant and has forgotten the gift."

Understanding this was another powerful turning point for me!

My clients and colleagues who have the most trouble with this are those who have gotten through life largely due to their strong minds. This shift can be challenging for them, at first, and then it can change their whole world in the most profound ways.

I tell people that I do not allow my mind to make any decisions for me. Often, the first reaction to that is a blank stare followed by a "WHAT?!" It's true. Allowing my mind to make my decisions is like letting a five-year-old run my business and my life. I give my mind work to do that it is best suited for. I use it as the tool it is meant to be.

The decisions I have made guided by inspiration are always far more successful than the decisions I have made guided by my data. It's a muscle, and it has to be strengthened. It requires a huge shift in your perspective and the way you process.

It also requires Trust. I talk a lot about my journey being a journey of Trust x 3: Trust Yourself, Trust Divine Intelligence, Trust the Process. It will be the same for you when you decide to give it a go living this way. One thing I am going to do is to teach you how to recognize the synchronicities and signs along the way that are always provided and how to follow the breadcrumbs and respond to the opportunities. Once you see this is there for you, and you learn to read the feedback that is always there, you will be able to come along much further into your Trust.

Trust is super important to start cultivating, because, as you build the life you desire and call in all the things you need and want, you will be letting go of a lot, as well. You will be led to release ways of being, and doing, of having and not having, that no longer serve you. You will be observing your thoughts, feelings, and actions and considering your current beliefs about everything. You will start seeing things differently, and hearing things you have never been able to hear before. You will discover what roles you have been playing that are for the benefit of others but not for you. You will choose to step into new roles that better reflect who you are and offer you the opportunity for fuller and more fulfilling self-expression.

Know this, your changing will be inconvenient and uncomfortable for others in your life. Besides you fighting yourself internally, others will buck up against you. Some who you expect to be there for you won't be, and some you would never expect will show up fully for you. This is the time you will need to really start learning to trust yourself, trust Divine Intelligence, and trust the process. I am going to arm you with the tools you need to navigate this journey. It will begin with your decision to embark on it.

A REFLECTION FOR YOU: The Hero Setting Out on Her Journey

This traveler hears the calling and has gotten up to take a step, to move forward, to take a new inspired action. Somewhere within, she knows that this step will lead her into the unknown, away from the comfortable and the familiar, defying what has come to be considered logical and rational.

The Hero's Journey all begins from this place, from our position as the Innocent. In this place, many of us have experienced feelings of going crazy, and others may tell us we are acting foolish. Yet, we stand up and take that first step, which changes the energy within us. It changes everything. We declare something new to the Universe, and indeed the Universe does respond.

She travels light, as she has begun to let go of many things. As we embark on this part of the Journey, we are asked to let go of everything that does not serve us and make room for all that we are asking for and expectantly waiting for to show up.

In her humanness, she gives way to her feelings and emotions, experiences her desires, reaches for what she wants, and then creates the space for life to happen, for Divine Intelligence to join with human in this creative process, in this dance, and lets go of the outcome to allow what is meant to be simply to be. It is a delicate balance, this way. Of being. Of experiencing life. It is in the moment of surrender that the zero point exists, the event horizon, the void in which all is possible and creations are made manifest.

Don't let this frighten you away. Some people will choose to abandon much of the life they are dissatisfied with, take big risks, giant steps forward. Part of the Wisdom within is that it calls you first and foremost to "Know Thyself." This is what the journey is truly all about. I tell my clients and students that they must know themselves well enough to know what is best for them. These choices will impact them physically, mentally, emotionally, and spiritually; wholly. If you are not a risk taker then taking big risks can create stress that counteracts and interferes with your ability to create what you are wanting. This movement can take the form of baby steps. Small, subtle consistent actions will create profound change. The important thing is to get into action and stay in action. It is an art that can be mastered.

Everyone and every place is open to her right now. At the beginning of the journey, standing in this place, all possibilities exist simultaneously.

Today, spend some time reflecting or meditating on this message that she offers us, this gift that she brings.

> *When you change your mind about what's possible*
> *for your life, your life will rise up to meet you."*
> —Kris Carr

A Letter to the Universe Tool for You

I'd like you to write what we refer to in the Loving What's Next Coaching Program as A Letter to the Universe. This is a letter to Spirit or Soul or God or Source or Higher Self, whatever language speaks to you.

In this letter, what I would like you to do is pour out your heart on all the things that are in your awareness right now. Allow new awareness to emerge.

I would like you to share your Vision with the Universe and share WHY you want this Vision for yourself and what it will bring to your life or your family or the world.

Then I would like you to share with the Universe what would most support you in achieving your Vision. What would most support you in gaining clarity and moving you forward?

Now, here's the most important part—write any fear, concerns, or doubts you have about any piece of moving forward, of moving beyond where you are into a new, higher energy pattern in your life. Really release those fears.

Literally, release it and let it go . . . hand it over to the Universe.

So often, we can believe the things that are coming up for us are real, when in reality it is just fear presenting itself, "FEAR: False Evidence Appearing Real." Fear is really just energy—not reality.

The most important part is that I want you to hand over any fears, doubts, or concerns. It might sound something like this: "Dear Universe, I want to hand this over to you. I'm so afraid that . . . but, I recognize that you are much more powerful than anything that I could do on my own, so I release this to you . . ." or, however that might sound to you, speaking from your heart and your Soul.

Release, let go, and be open to receiving a sign.

This is a powerful process, so get it down on paper and out of your head. Really take the time to experience this for yourself.

Ask the Universe to open up possibilities that you can't even see right now, and then turn it over, literally, surrender it. And then what I'd like you to do is open yourself up to signs about the next best steps for you. Open yourself up to new information and new perspectives. We all receive signs differently. Some people hear things, some get a visual. Some people actually see a sign, some have a knowing. It's different for each person. Simply open yourself up to possibilities and ask for a sign of what is the next best step for you.

Put this letter away for three days, seventy-two hours, then come back and read it again, reflect on it and journal anything additional that comes up for you. Put this letter away again, and do not open it up until six months or a year later. You will be amazed when you read it again how well you can see and understand everything that has gone on over those months and shown up in your life. You can use this tool over and over again.

CHAPTER 2

Are You Ready for the Trust Fall?

This happens to me a lot. I get contacted by people I have heard from before. I recognize them from my community, they may have come and heard me speak somewhere, they may follow me on social media, saw me on tv, or read one of my books, and they are attracted to what I am sharing with them and what they believe I am saying to them. Something in them is telling them that I can help, and they so want what I am saying to be true. Yet, they come and go, and they never make a decision, and they never commit. I may not see or hear from them for up to a year, then they come back again, still drawn, still speaking to their desires and dreams, and they ask me, how, how can I make this happen? I want to, but . . .

Here is what I have to tell you. It is about making a decision and making a commitment to yourself, then watching for the opportunities to show up to create the means to make it happen. As long as you are holding the energy and coming from the place of, I will when . . . you will continue to wait until . . . there just really is no substitute for deciding to do it. I remember some of my first uncertain steps and being so scared; how was I going to make this happen, could I count on this even being true, and, even so, how would I know it would work for me?

I see this so often, and I really wish I had another answer, I really wish I could tell you to just sit tight and the money will come streaming in. When? When the Divine Intelligence feels you are ready? You tell the Divine Intelligence when you are ready. We are promised freewill on this planet, and Divine Intelligence, although all powerful and omniscient, will not impede on your free will. When Divine Intelligence thinks you can handle it? If the desire exists within you, then the means to attain it is already here, it already exists. When things are better? When you are stronger? You get better and stronger by being in it, by doing it and growing and evolving along with what you are creating. It is a totally organic process, and you have to be engaged in it for it to work. Are you waiting until you are more prepared, have made time for it, cleared your major obligations, don't have so much you need to do for everybody else? You will always have things in your life, and stuff will always come up. These things show up over and over again as a response, as a match to the energy you are holding in your thoughts, beliefs, actions, and repeated patterns.

So, what are you really waiting for?

I'd like to share an experience with you that I had in hopes that I can give you a true feel for what the energy feels like that will get you there. I want you to understand what energy you need to hold to make it happen. In my M.O.V.E. process, which I will share with you in depth in this book, I start everything with having you

Make A Decision and then owning it 100 percent. And there's a reason for that.

When I'm talking about making that decision and owning it, visualizing it, and executing it, I want to give you this example. It was so powerful. I love how it showed up.

A friend of mine was doing this extreme confidence boot camp, and I was one of the teachers in it. I love when I'm the teacher and, of course, I get to be the student, and I get to be challenged. I get the opportunity to walk my talk. I love how that is.

Part of this involved this ropes course, and I had no fear about it. They had this two-story building with a set up, and you're up on tight ropes, you're harnessed, there's zip lines, you're walking on all these obstacles. I had no fear about any of that.

There's one thing I had tremendous fear and doubt about, and that was the trust fall. A big part of this kind of boot camp is to show you that the way you do anything is the way you do everything, and it all shows up. You learn physically, mentally, emotionally really by going through these different exercises and working with that group dynamic. What you really feel in the world and how you show up in the world will show up in this experience. I surprised myself with this trust fall; it just terrified me. And it was beautiful, because we did it right before I was to teach this exact thing that I'm presenting now.

I had given this talk many times, all over, about mastering the art of taking action, about making a decision, the importance of committing fully to it and supporting yourself 100 percent, and this day I was giving this talk. So, the instructor said, "It's time for the trust fall." Basically, everyone in your group is standing in two lines facing each other and just holding out their arms. We were a group of mostly women that day. There are these steps leading up to this platform, and you are going to climb up the steps, turn your back to the group, and they've created this cradle with their arms, and you are going to fall backwards into their arms. Very quickly, I realized several things.

I told you, I'm a huge risk taker. I don't mind taking risks, but with the risks I take, I'm counting on myself. I know I have everything I need, and I have everything in place, so this, to me, felt like a risk I wasn't sure I wanted to take. I can't even see the people, I don't know if they're going to catch me, I believe they have the intention to catch me, I trust them that much. But I don't know if they will. Can you begin to see how this might have played out first in my early life then continued as I carried this energy with me?

I've been bonding with them all day. I don't know if they can catch me, and I don't know if I want to count on that. Suddenly, it was a risk I did not want to take. I'm falling backwards into the unknown. All these things started coming up for me, and when I started teaching this material afterwards, it all came together.

I want you to think about this. I let a lot of people go ahead of me, not knowing if I would even do this at all, and when she told me it was my turn, "Michelle you're doing this," I had not yet made the decision. In that moment, part of it was that pressure of, I'm getting ready to teach these people something, all eyes are on me. It was a beautiful chance for me to be vulnerable in a powerful way and make it a teaching moment while I was experiencing it myself.

In this moment, I made the decision. Going up those steps, I still did not know if I was truly going to do this, if I had it in me. But there comes a point where you have to make a decision, and this is the part I really want you to understand. Climbing up those steps, I was saying, "Yeah, there are going to be some consequences if I choose not to do it. Nothing bad is going to happen to me, but I really want to come through for myself, I really want to do this, and I feel like I need to do it."

You need to get comfortable with getting uncomfortable, and that's something I'm always telling my clients and students, so guess what? Again, I have to walk my talk. They were all getting uncomfortable in all kinds of ways throughout the day. This was my moment. When you get to the top, you turn away from the crowd, and they have given you this very specific way you have to stand. You have to cross your arms, you have to straighten your body, your legs have to be a certain way, and your feet, and you assume this position before you fall.

Right then and there, I had to make a decision and own it, and then I had to visualize myself doing it, and then I'm going to execute it. All of this happened in a matter of minutes. There was no room for second guessing or doubting, because once you make the decision and you start that momentum backwards, which is, you start the action, if you come out of that position, you're going to hurt the people who are trying to catch you, you're going to hurt yourself, and it becomes dangerous. Perfect setup for me. It was a moment where, once I made the decision, I had to support myself 100 percent. There was no way to stop myself once I set this in motion. I knew that. I could feel it the moment I got into this position, and I said, "In a moment, I'm going to fall backwards. I cannot stop myself."

Once I start falling, I cannot say, oh, not doing this, and if I let anything get in my way and I come out of the position, I'm going to hurt people that are trusting me, and I'm going to get hurt. I took so much from that about this moving forward work I am teaching you now. What a great way to really get it. I think of that every time I'm going to make a decision now—then I own it, visualize it and execute it 100 percent as if there is no turning back and no stopping mid-air.

You have got to do it at 100 percent. If you come in and out of it, it's damaging. It's damaging to you, it's damaging to the other people involved.

What if you went into everything you did in that way?

Without all the push-pull energy, the in then out energy, the stopping and starting energy. I really want you to think about the commitment. And if commitment is an issue for you, if it feels scary, if you can't hold it for a long period of time, commit for an hour, commit for twenty-four hours, just start committing and stick with it.

What are you ready to do this with right now? That's your starting point.

Now is the time to start. It's always the time to start. Wherever you are, whatever your life and world are about right now, you will know what your next steps are. Synchronicities will begin to occur if you open up to them. Someone, something will show up and open you up and positively charge you, and you will have the opportunity to step into it.

You showed up here, now, for a reason. You have desires that are speaking to you, dreams that are calling to you. But you don't see how you can make that happen, especially not right now.

I have some clients who really resonate when I talk to them about doing a Trust Fall into the lap of Divine Intelligence. They are the ones who are able to move forward fast and create what they need, want, and desire.

> *Hold the vision, drop the excuses and remember your why.*
> *Swerve around obstacles, and trust the process.*
> *Happiness and success will find you.*
> —Karen Salmansohn

CHAPTER 3

Are You Willing to Let Go of What No Longer Serves You?

Achieving the success that you desire is always much more about what you are willing to do than what you can do. You can always find help with that. It's everywhere. So, begin by getting honest with yourself. It's time for what we call in my community, Taking Honest Inventory. Get clear on what is in front of you to do that you are not doing.

Before we get to the doing of it, we have to determine why we aren't doing it. That's the real work.

There are times in my life when I didn't have the strategies and the know-how to do the things that would get the results I desired. Especially early on in the building of the business that now supports and sustains the life I desire to live. Many more times, I had to become the person who could get those results. I began to hire the coaches, teachers, and mentors who could give me what I didn't have, show me and tell me what I didn't know. Then, I realized that there were some things they would give me that I would run with and some things I wouldn't. I am an action taker and have learned to be even more so since discovering the power in taking aligned inspired action. Yet, some strategies and solutions would be right there in front of me. They were clear, they were proven, and, still, I wasn't doing them. That's when I had to take honest inventory about what I was willing to do and where what I was not willing to do was greatly impacting my life.

As I grew and transformed, I saw how the work I did with my clients was dependent to a large degree on how I could guide and support them to become the person who gets the results they need and want. I worked with this concept more and more for myself as I worked more and more on this with my clients.

Along with determining why we aren't doing those things that will bring us what we are asking for, we have to become very good at determining why we are doing a lot of other things that are causing us to self-sabotage and derail our results, along with our relationships, our money, our health, and our businesses and careers, until our life feels out of control and not at all what we expected.

Here is an analogy I share often with my clients. You walk along toward what you desire, and suddenly you come to a wall. You stand there, thinking and feeling things, deciding what action to take, and you are stuck. You decide you are not supported in what you want and need, you cannot do this right now, or you cannot do this at all. You start telling a story about how this always happens to you, you never get a break, things outside of your control are always in your way. You say maybe another time, when I am feeling better, when I am stronger, when I have more support, when I have more money, when the circumstances are different.

But, you created these circumstances. Every time you get up and start walking forward toward what you desire, and you come to this place, the wall will be there. The wall is of your making. The time you are able to break through what stands in your way and move just a few steps beyond it, you will turn around and find that the wall is gone. It no longer exists. And that wall will never block your path again.

There is a Zen Proverb that says, "The obstacle is the path." After experiencing this myself, I have gone on to teach my clients and students that, whatever you believe is in the way is the way.

Let that land.

A TOOL FOR YOU: Eliminate Your Tolerations

Here is an exercise I was asked to do by a coach of mine that I ended up working with for three and a half years. This was early on in my entrepreneurial journey, and this exercise became a very powerful tool for me that I would love to see you utilize, as well. Commit to doing it once, now, and then add it to your toolbox to use over and over again, at least once a year.

I was asked by my coach to make a list of "50 Things I Am Tolerating in My Life." Things we tolerate but give attention to use a portion of our vital life force energy. We think and feel about them, we talk about them, we get ready to get ready to do something about them. These tolerations can be large or small in scope; they can be anything from a squeaky door to a toxic relationship, and everything in between. Whatever we focus on persists. Where our attention goes, our energy flows. We alert our subconscious mind that this is important, and it sets out to keep bringing it up in front of us to solve the problem. I used to be one to put things off to deal with later so that I could attend to what I considered the most important and pressing matters in front of me. But, when I started using this tool, I saw how much energy was freed up by eliminating these tolerations, and how much more ease and swiftness I experienced in creating the things I needed, wanted, and desired.

When you are available for things that bother you, frustrate you, anger you, irritate you, and hurt and harm you, your energy becomes a match to more of the same. As you give attention and energy to them, they grow and become magnetic. Your emotions are energy in motion. You have energy leaks and energy drains that drag you down and wear you out. It takes a lot of energy to create what you desire.

I learned to use a powerful mantra I will share with you. Any time I became aware of something I was allowing myself to be available for that no longer served me and that I did not want to be available for, and when I saw how it was holding away from me the very things I needed, wanted, and desired, I began to say to myself and out loud, "I am no longer available for . . ." As this worked better and better for me, I started having my clients do it, too.

1. Begin by examining what you tolerate. Take honest inventory.
2. Make a list of fifty things you are tolerating in your life. Reach deep and wide.
3. Commit to eliminating your tolerations. Take both baby steps and ledge leaps. Some of these will require only one step and others will be progress in the making. And they will stretch and grow you.

Deciding what you want and creating what you want is just as much about deciding what you are no longer available for and learning how to stop creating what you don't want.

A REFLECTION FOR YOU: Why Am I Creating What I Don't Want?

Think about it. That's a very different question than, Why Am I Not Creating What I Want? For really, there's no "not creating" about it. You are the Creator of your entire life, of your entire experience. Things don't happen to us, they happen through us.

I have always been able to create some things I wanted, but I didn't always understand what I was doing consciously, so I spent a lot of years creating a lot of what I didn't want, as well.

Why Am I Creating What I Don't Want?

Divine Intelligence doesn't listen to your words and obey them. Divine Intelligence responds to your vibration, to what you are sending out through your thoughts which create feelings, and it is your feelings that are magnetic and attract to you a match to what you are sending out.

Imagine that you are sending out to Divine Intelligence a strong desire for the love of your life. You want it. You know you want it. You are sending this desire out into the Universe. Chances are, because you have such strong desire, you also have some resistance to your desire because of your attachment to it, your limiting beliefs, your bad habits and unhealthy patterns, and your toxic emotions. As you are sending out your desire for the love of your life—you can feel it, you can see it, you have made your list about all the qualities you want it to show up with—you have to be aware of what else is going out in your request. Because what you say is, IS. Remember that Divine Intelligence will not impede on our free will.

Things that might get into the mix could include, "I've been hurt before. I am afraid to get hurt again," or, "I think I'm ready to open my heart and my life to someone else, but I'm not sure I'm ready. Am I really ready?" Unworthiness could be getting broadcast out in your request, along with not good enough, not enough, or fear, doubt, and guilt. The possibilities are endless, and most often we are unconscious of them, and yet they hold so much power in our creating.

Have you made room for your creation to show up—really, really made room? Divine Intelligence responds to a true vacuum and comes in to answer true need. If you are holding onto things and people that no longer serve you waiting for this new creation of your dreams to show up, it won't.

When it comes to creating, we operate on a continuum of conscious and unconscious creation, and at any given time we can be creating from anywhere along that continuum. If you picture yourself on this continuum with 0 percent to 100 percent, from unconscious creating to conscious creating, it is beneficial for you to increase your awareness of the energetic dynamic at play here. How much of the time are you creating unconsciously? This results in a lot of mis-creating and a lot of what you don't want showing up in the process. Now, how much of the time are you consciously creating, showing up as a co-creative partner with Divine Intelligence? THIS results in much more creating what you DO want.

How do I become more conscious and create more of what I need, want, and desire?

These are the 9 Universal Guiding Principles for My Business and My Life, the way I do my part and allow Divine Intelligence to work in my favor:

1. Energy flows where attention goes. What we resist persists. Pay close attention to what you are focusing on. What are you thinking about? What are you feeling? How much time are you spending focusing on what you want, and how much time are you spending focusing on what you don't want?

2. Everything counts. Everything matters. A choice point exists in every moment. Our life is shaped by the series of choices we make along the way. Become more conscious about the choices presented to you. Become more conscious of your ability to choose. This requires a shift in perspective from Victim to Creator. This requires taking complete responsibility for all of it.

3. Everything is Energy. You are an energetic being in energetic exchange with Divine Intelligence and everyone and everything in the Universe. Become more aware of the energy you are directing outward through your thoughts, feelings, and actions, and shift what no longer serves you through your own healing and transformation to create your extraordinary life. Learn to work with this. Everything that shows up in your life is there for a reason. You can learn to interpret this, recognize it, heal and clear it, and create life YOUR way.

4. When we begin to dream big dreams, to set intentions and goals for ourselves, when we begin to strive for a more extraordinary life, everything that is not in alignment with that rises up to be healed or transformed. I call that, "Your stuff coming up." When you step into your intentions, dreams and goals, your "stuff" is going to come up. You can choose to heal and clear this so that you can move forward and step out of mediocrity into your most extraordinary expression and experience.

5. Learn to leave the "hows" to Divine Intelligence. Get to the essence of what you want. Dream big. See it, feel it, live it, love it, be it. Don't waste your time asking, how? "How could THIS possibly happen for ME?" Don't let your logical mind take over and try to figure it all out. That will take you right into stories of limitation, scarcity, and lack. Divine Intelligence can create miracles when we move out of the way.

6. Get out of your head and get out of your stories. We all have created stories we tell others and ourselves that define who we are and what our lives are about. These stories have power over us. They are highly charged with words and emotions. We can become trapped within our stories. Start recognizing what stories you are telling, then stop telling your stories.

7. The Laws of the Universe are always on. They always exist, just like natural laws, whether you believe in them or not, whether you are actively working with them or not. It is not something you can spend time on here and there and get consistent results. A common misperception I see people

making is that they set aside some time to meditate or journal or say their affirmations or attend a workshop, and then
they step right back into living their life with their limiting
beliefs, bad habits and unhealthy patterns, and toxic emotions driving their bus. And then they wonder why Divine
Intelligence is not working in their favor.

8. Once you start taking aligned and inspired action, don't
stop. Act, Assess and Adjust. Keep going. So many people
stop just short of taking action. They hesitate, and then
they miss the moment Divine Intelligence has stepped in
to meet them. You can learn to stay connected to Source/
Creator and to receive inspiration. Then it's still up to you
to ACT.

9. Before the doing comes the being. This one is counterin-
tuitive to a lot of people when they first start working with
it. Many people come for help, and they say, tell me what
to do, and I'll do it . . . if you can guarantee that I'll get
these results. They say that when they have something, they
will do something that will allow them to be something. It
doesn't work that way. You have to be the thing you want
to be first. You have to do the things that people like that
would do. And THEN you will have what people like that
have. We call this the Be-Do-Have.

Principles, once applied, become more than a way of doing
things. They become a way of living, a way of being. The more you
learn to work with Divine Intelligence according to the Universal
Laws, the less action you are required to engage in. You begin to
attract to you everything you need. Things begin to come together

more easily and effortlessly in a way that you know is coming from Divine Intelligence.

If you like these and want them in front of you, you can download as my gift to you, *The 9 Universal Guiding Principles* at www.9universalguidingprinciples.com.

Now, what is the most important thing you need to do? Show up! This is key. Show up now and in every moment, a ready and willing partner with Divine Intelligence, excited to co-create. Show up, and trust that you already have everything you need. Show up for yourself now.

I want you to be excited about your journey. You notice I didn't say get excited; I said BE excited! Your journey is now, always. You are on it, always have been. We need to stop holding the energy of "gonna" and "getting to" something. Here's a secret! There is no failure; there are no mistakes. The more you begin to consciously create, follow the inspiration into aligned inspired action, and the more you learn to Act, Assess, and Adjust, the more you learn to make course corrections that save you a lot of time and energy and spare you a lot of pain.

Pain happens. Suffering is optional. Helen Keller said, "Life is either a daring adventure or nothing." You CAN walk through life engaged in your own process. You CAN become more conscious and create more of what you need, want, and desire?

I see the truth that lives within you. I hold the grandest vision of the greatest version of you. I see your gifts. And, I see how you are holding yourself back. Now is the perfect time to create your extraordinary life, to transcend self-imposed limits and break free from mis-creating unconsciously. You have everything inside of you in this moment that you need. There are no failures, no mistakes. You are on your path, always, and this is your journey. You get to choose what step you will take next. Your WHOLE Life Is Waiting. What are YOU waiting for? I invite you to explore your own unlimited possibilities. I invite you to take inspired action, to step out of mediocrity and create your own extraordinary life.

It takes courage to grow up and become who you really are.
—c. e. cummings

CHAPTER 4

Are You Done with Confusion?

I want to ask you this, "How is your confusion currently serving you?"

Confusion. It's one of the things I most often see keeping people stuck. Whenever you get stuck in Confusion, the first thing you want to do is to remember your touchstone, your Vision. The clearer your Vision, the easier it is to make decisions and choices, because each choice you come to is an opportunity to make a decision that will either move you toward or away from your Vision.

Ask yourself, "What is my priority right now? What can I do right now to make this happen?"

Go back to your Vision, and then go back to the question, and that will help you get out of Confusion when you are faced with all these different pieces, remembering that everything moves you either away from or toward your Vision. Every day, you will have decisions. There will be choice points in every moment, and the more you are aware of this, you won't get stuck in it. You will keep moving forward. Keep doing this until it becomes easier, until it becomes more natural in a flow and habit.

At first, it's like training, like an Olympic athlete having to train. You're really having to rewire yourself physiologically, you're having to reset your mindset. You're having to reset the mode of whether you're responding or reacting. You're having to reset the way you interact with your environment and the people and the things in your environment. Know that this is a process.

Get very good at being willing to stop and make that change and make that shift. Keep revisiting your Vision. At first, when you wake up every morning, make it a habit, make it a part of your success plan, your personal success strategy, to bring that Vision to mind and recommit yourself to it and then move forward into your day.

That way, it's on top of your mind. You've programmed your subconscious to understand exactly what to be looking for, because you've said, "Here's what I want. Here's my big Vision." We have millions of bits of information that come into our sensory perception throughout every day, and you have a reticular activating system in your body that says, "Pay attention to this; don't pay attention to that."

A lot of time, when we're getting a lot of Confusion, we start asking questions, and questions are very good in the right energy. What we tend to do is get into a state of constriction, where we're almost folding in over ourselves and asking questions.

Sometimes, we're asking questions that aren't helping. "Why? Why is this always happening to me? Why can't I make it work? What's going on here? I don't know what to do." It creates constricting energy. It brings forward the constriction of everything within us. You do not want to get into that space.

What you want to do is come into a state of expansion where you're asking open-ended questions. Again, when you're asking, "Why is this always happening to me?" The Universe will always answer any question, anything you send out, and those tend to have a lot of energy, a lot of feeling behind them. What you'll get is consistent evidence of why this is happening to you. What that's going to look like is more and more lessons, more and more of what you believe always happens to you, never happens to you, whatever it is.

When you ask, "Why is this always happening to me? Why can't I?," you're asking for feedback. The Universe is going to give it to you, and it's going to look like more of what you don't want.

So, when you stop and you get into a state of expansion, you want to ask questions that the Universe can bring you answers to. You want to say, "What is possible? What could be better? What could be more? How can I make an impact today? How can I make more money today? How can I be in a more loving relationship today?"

Whatever you are asking, the Universe is answering, so keeping yourself in a state of Confusion is always a choice. There is something you are refusing to see, or there is something you are refusing to respond to. It's there. Wherever there is a need and a desire, there is also the ability to fulfill it. Now.

When you are faced with Confusion, a couple of things are going on. The first thing you do is say, "Oh, this is Confusion." You can choose to stay in a confused state. I will tell you, if you're staying in a confused state for any length of time, you're choosing to do that, and it's serving you. Then, you need to go back and take honest inventory and figure out why you are needing to stay in this state.

When faced with Confusion, there is always something you can do to move out of Confusion.

One, your Purpose is not clear enough, and you are not attached enough to it. You haven't bought into it. You can't envision it enough. You're not fully there, or you don't fully believe it can happen. You don't have a strong enough "Why?"

Go back, at this point, to your Purpose, Vision and Why, and work on these things. Explore your Vision. Explore your Mission. Explore your Dreams, and explore your Truth. Your Purpose is the fuel. The Confusion is the brakes.

Another thing that can be going on is that you have a conflict within you. You may not be aware of it. It's very likely you aren't. You are not in alignment in all levels of your awareness.

Parts of you are on board. Inside of you, you have all these different levels of awareness, and there are parts of you that are not buying into the Vision and are not going there, because they have determined some level of it not being safe or not being comfortable, or there's a belief that's getting in the way. These beliefs can be getting in the way and putting on the brakes.

The other thing that can be going on is that there is something you don't know. You get into confusion, and you get overwhelmed. "I lack the skills. I lack the resources." In this case, determine what is going on and what you need to know to move forward. If this is the case, ask yourself, "Hey, what do I need to know?" "Do I really not know?" This is where you start chunking it down, if it feels really big.

Just start with, "What is one thing I need to know?" and then take an action in that direction.

Be willing to take a look at yourself and see which of these things is going on. Take 100 percent responsibility to push through your Confusion. Recognize it as Resistance. Once you determine which of these things is going on, you need to sit down and say, "What do I need to do right now?" You know. By now, you know what you need to do next. And, then, you ask yourself this, and this is where the rubber meets the road, "Am I willing to do this?"

I cannot tell you how many people, and you will know this is true, how many people know exactly what they need to do next, and they're just not doing it. They keep saying, "I don't know what to do next," or, "I can't do what I need to do next." "I don't have the time." "I don't have the money." "I don't know where to start."

It's that simple. Because once you get honest with yourself, and you start asking yourself these questions and answering them, Boom! "What do I need to do next?" "I know this is what I need to do next." "Am I willing to do this, yes or no?" Yes? Okay, now you know what you need to do next! No? Okay, now you are being honest, and you really aren't confused at all.

And now you are getting Clarity, and that is the first step to move you forward in the direction of your dreams and desires to create a better life now!

If your answer here is "No," then it's time to go back to emotional mastery, energy management, intuitive development, and taking honest inventory. These are all aspects of my programs.

Regardless, you keep working through it. You don't stop. If you're asking yourself questions, you take it to deeper and deeper levels. You don't get stuck in Confusion.

If it's too big, you chunk it down. You chunk it way down. You chunk it way, way down, and you seek help and guidance when you need it.

"I'm confused. I'm stuck." is an excuse. Confusion is a defense mechanism. It does not serve you. It creates a story, and allows you to live in that story, if you choose. It is a distraction, and it is ultimately avoidance.

Recognize it. Own it. Push through Resistance into Receptivity. Get started right now.

CHAPTER 5

Are You Excited to Reconnect with Your Own True Desires?

D o you trust your desires? I do.

No matter where you are when you come to me, I always go straight to your desires, because these come from your Soul, your Higher Self, and your knowing, and they are always the way forward, even when, and especially when you don't know how. Not knowing the how stops many people in their tracks. Universal Law says, "Leave the how's to the Universe," and that has been some of the best and most helpful guidance I have ever received and that I can give my clients and students.

The minute you connect with your true desires and really start to envision them, to feel and experience them, and dare to hope they could become a reality, your mind comes in with a fear response, asking, "But how . . ."; "How could that work . . ."; and "That can't work, can it?" Along with, "And it would take a

43

long time . . ."; "And I don't have the time . . ."; "I don't have the money . . ."; or "Insert your biggest excuse here!"

This is all natural and normal, and it is a distraction, an interference, a safety mechanism at the level of your mind. What you need to know is, IT DOES NOT SERVE YOU.

In order to work with your desires, you have to do the mindset work, the energy management, the emotional mastery, and not let your mind get in the way. Your mind can be used later, for a lot of things. Right now, it's not needed, and letting your mind run the show right now is like letting a five-year old run your life or your business.

The Ego has a lot of tricks up its sleeve. Confusion. Forgetfulness. Distraction. Procrastination. Drama. And it will throw a temper tantrum like a two-year old when you are getting closest to the change you desire. #SoulTeach.

Visioning Your What's Next Tool: Five minutes a day for thirty days

Start right now by spending five minutes a day completely immersed in your Vision. This does not require hours of meditation. Consistently spend five minutes a day as often as you can envisioning all aspects of your desired life and experience. Don't get caught up in the How's. What does your world look like? What is around you? What are you doing? Where are you living? Focus on all five senses and imagine your life as you desire it. The most important thing to ask yourself is, What do you feel like? How does living your life and having all that you desire feel to you? Give words to those feelings, and feel them in your body, in your heart, in your solar plexus where your knowing resides. At first, you might feel that you are imagining these things or working to conjure them up. The more you can start training yourself to feel rather than think, the better off you will be and the more you will be able to harness your power to create. As you continue to do this, you will begin to step into this world of your inner creation, and you will see and feel things showing up that might surprise you. Take some time at the end of each visioning session to make some notes or write in a journal. Become hyper alert to everything that is showing up in your outer world. Watch for signs and synchronicities, notice things that are a match to your desires and that have been in your visioning exercises. As the breadcrumbs begin to appear, follow them. As the opportunities start to show up, say Yes to them. Do this for thirty days, and watch what happens!

You will most of the time be shown only the next step. Understand this is because you have freewill, you have a choice point in every moment. Everything matters, and everything counts. Once you make a decision and take an action, all energy shifts to the new reality moving either toward or away from what you desire. You are choosing in every moment by your thoughts, feelings, and action to move either toward or away from what you want. Bring this into your conscious awareness. Your energetic stance is recorded, and it ripples out to everyone and everything involved in the manifestation of your desire. Then, the next breadcrumb to follow or opportunity to step into shows up.

Too many people never take any action toward what they say they want most, and then they wonder why they don't have it.

So many people come to me and say they will take action or say yes to something if they can have guarantees and know all the steps. This will never happen. It shifts energetically as you are in it.

You are the catalyst. You have freewill, and that means, you always have to go first. The Universe, Creator, Source, Spirit, God cannot impede on your freewill. You always have to go first. Then, Spirit will rush in to meet you with all manner of help. The Universe does not play the when/then game. We came here for the experience. A perfect plan does not pre-exist; it becomes as we grow and evolve. It's an organic process, and it's miraculous.

> *The Universe responds to action. The Universe steps in to meet true need. The Universe does not play the when/then game. #SoulTeach.*

Be aware when the things you are visioning in your inner world start to take form in your outer world. This is feedback, and it's very valuable. The things that show up are a match to you right now. Everything that shows up that you want is a signal to you that you are already a match to it. Nothing is currently getting in the way around this. The things that show up that you don't want are signaling you to pay attention, this is what needs to be cleared, healed, and resolved for you to receive what you are asking for. Ask and it is given is in every sacred text. It is Universal Law. The minute you start asking, your desires are on their way to you. Now, your job is to become a match to them. These things need to be cleared, healed, and resolved to clear the way.

Imagine you are sending out an order to the Universe, so you want to become very aware and conscious. Whatever you get back tells you what you are sending out. Think of ordering a pizza. So, yes, if you have fears, those are emotions—energy in motion—and they go out in your order. So, you will see that reflected back. How helpful when you see it come back at you that you can recognize it and say, this is my fear, and it's not necessary, and it's not real, and I choose not to see that or expect that anymore, and then it can go away. Instead, we often react, and then tell a big story and make it worse, because the story you tell has to be.

You are learning to see what shows up and read the feedback and course correct. Act. Assess. Adjust. You are the Creator.

And no beating yourself up when that stuff shows up. It's actually the gold. It shows you what needs to be cleared, healed, and resolved so the Universe can deliver to you what you are telling it you want to be, do, and have. You see? So, clean it up. Everything you want is on the other side of it. But we get stopped by it.

The Universe always delivers what you are asking for. Ask and it is given is Universal Law and found in every sacred text.

The Universe starts delivering, and you will first see your "stuff," everything in the way of you receiving what you are asking for. Those are the tools for transformation. And they are actually a sign that you are on the right track! Reframe it. #SoulTeach.

You order your pizza, and here it comes to you, with everything you ordered on it. The pizza that is coming to you right now includes everything you are ordering right now with your vibration, your thoughts, your emotions—energy in motion. Wait, what about all this stuff I don't want? Yep, you are ordering that, too, only subconsciously.

It is more important than ever to consciously create rather than to let unconscious creating drive your bus. You are creating 24/7. How much of it is conscious? What shows up in your life that you don't want tells you what needs to be cleared, healed, and resolved so you can receive what you do want.

Start gaining awareness about what you are ordering up, then be the Creator of your own life, and order a new pizza. Read the feedback that shows up after your ASK. Clear, heal, and resolve what is in the way. Notice where you are already on track. Say, Yes, I love this! Give me more of this. Amplify how it makes you feel. Keep going, and don't stop, until it's here. (Hint, this is where the stories your mind wants to tell can really knock you off course and defeat you. I have a whole section on that for you. Don't miss it.)

There is an ancient proverb that says, The obstacle is the path. I teach it like this—whatever you think is in the way IS the way. This is another huge aha that was game-changing and life-changing for me.

You have a desire, and you decide to pursue it. You start your journey, moving toward your desire. At some time, you come to a wall. You might stand there awhile. You start thinking of all the reasons you need to retreat, right now. Your mind tells you, you can always come back later, when the time is better, when you have more money, when other people are more comfortable with this, insert your reason here.

The only thing standing between you and all that you desire is the Soul-crushing story you keep telling yourself about why you can't have it. #SoulTeach.

(There are those stories again!)

Here is a choice point, in this moment. The way to everything you desire is on the other side of this wall. This wall is built of fears, thoughts, feelings, stories that don't serve you, your mind trying to protect you, generational trauma, your own personal crisis and trauma that has not been healed, and a bunch of crap you have been programmed and conditioned with by family, culture, and society.

When you have a big vision, a mission calling to you, a purpose for being here on this planet that you are not expressing, and dreams for something better, it will eat away at you over time. You will become more and more disappointed, discouraged, discontent, restless, and disconnected from who you really are, and from the Divine Intelligence that connects you to your Higher Self and feeds and supports you into your greatness.

That desert I lived in for way too long was one of my own making. I know that now. Wandering around, I allowed myself to stay stuck in confusion as a coping mechanism, a protective device, and I got nowhere. I cried and ranted and railed against everyone and everything else. I cried out. I was stuck. I had lost touch with myself, I had forgotten my greatness and lost the motivation to pursue and live it. I found so many reasons why I could not, would not, should not pursue my purpose right here, right now. I made promises to myself that I didn't keep. It ate me alive from the inside out, and my life, every area of my life, reflected that back to me..

Something very important was hiding just behind my resistance to making a commitment to myself to step into who I am and take that out into the world. I couldn't see it. My choice point was there, in every moment, and every choice I made, every action I took or didn't take defined my life.

The moment I committed to myself and to that greater something, everything changed. My perspective changed. Instead of making excuses, I started seeking results.

This is precisely where the magic happened!

I sounded the call. I engaged first. I set in motion all that was ready to rush in to be a part of my creation, the answers to what I said I needed, wanted, and desired, for my bigger life. I was ready for it.

This time, I did not turn and walk away from the wall. I broke through it. I got to the other side of it. I realized I lived through it, and the crushing fears no longer held the same power over me. When I turned around, that wall was no longer there. It had been an illusion of my own making.

Yes, there will be other walls to break through on my journey. I have encountered many more of them. But this one is gone. And each time I break through, I have come that much closer to my manifested desires.

Whatever you think is in the way IS the way. The obstacle is the path.

CHAPTER 6

Are You Open to Begin Your Journey to Your Next?

Now that we have created an awareness of what your mind is going to be doing as you reconnect with your desires and start moving forward toward your desired next level life, you can consciously create from a place of clarity and focus.

Step One, Trust Your Desires.

Your true desires are waiting for you, and they may need some excavating. Very likely, they have been buried under, not now, not yet, and all signs point to no, it just wasn't meant to be, along with other peoples' wants, needs, and expectations of you and for you.

Know this:

Your changing is going to be highly inconvenient and uncom-
fortable for some people in your life;
and
Spirit wants for you what you want for yourself. Spirit cre-
ated you to 'be a Creator, and Spirit gave you free will. It's all
here for you. You have to choose it. And you have to choose to
be the person who can be it, do it, and have it.

It is Universal Law: If you have a Desire, then a way has been made. It already exists.

Start here. Trust this. The journey you are on is a journey of Trustx3, learning to Trust Spirit, Trust Yourself, and trust the Process. Can you trust, right now, that if you have a desire, a way exists?

From this place, you can open up to the opportunities that show up when you ASK. They are there. They start appearing the moment you ASK. The problem is, you can't always see them, because they often appear uncomfortable, inconvenient, or even illogical. And you have to step in and say yes and follow the breadcrumbs. First, you have to recognize them when they show up.

So, do this, right now:

- Make a clear ASK to the Universe.
- Become hyper alert watching for the opportunities.
- Say "Yes!" and step in.
- Follow the breadcrumbs.

When a Desire enters your heart, a way has already been made. The Universe will rush in to guide and support you. You have to take the first step. Always.

Creating Your Desire Guide: A Working Document

Dare to desire out loud!

Grab a beautiful journal and pen or a simple spiral notebook, and start putting your desires on paper.

I know, we are a technology fueled age, and we have all the devices. Do what works best for you, but there is scientific proof that writing things down when manifesting your desires creates results through brain connection that isn't as proven using other methods. Give it a try.

Every day, for five minutes, visit your vision, and write down things you are aware that you desire. Let them bubble up. Let them surprise you.

Write them all into being, the very big, and the smallest. Watch as your desires grow clearer and as they shift and change as you work with them. It's okay to change your focus as you fully enter into the process.

Stop yourself from trying to control the how's and from any negative self-talk that comes in while you are working with your desires. It's all valuable feedback for you to work with. Write it down somewhere else so you can work with it, but not in your Desire Guide.

One version of this is known as Scripting. Using Scripting, you write it all out as a narrative in the present tense, as if you sat down with a friend for coffee that you hadn't seen in a while and wanted to catch her up on your whole life. You would speak with feeling. You would be animated. You would paint a picture for her. You would leave nothing wonderful out. Talk and write about the being, the doing, and the having.

I also used a form of Scripting often in my early days of creating the first version of my business and the life I desired by speaking it. I had a long driveway to the mailbox, and while I was walking it with my dogs, I would tell them out loud all the things I was so happy about that had shown up in my life. When I was driving, I would talk to myself out loud. Whenever a thought would come in that was negating all the great things that were on their way to me and already mine, I would speak what I desired into being, telling my mind what is.

It is Universal Law, Whatever you say is, IS. #SoulTeach.

(Yes, the stories you tell are a powerful tool in how this all goes! More about that soon.)

Write your desires in your book for five minutes every day for thirty days, and watch what happens!

As your desires are manifested, check them off in your book.

It is important that you make your ASK and turn them over to the Universe. Some things will show up very fast, because you are a clear match to them. Other desires will be taking form as you work with them. Some of my desires have shown up much later than I expected and turned out to be right on time. The Universe remembers all your desires and delivers them to you when you are a match to them.

Another version of the book is a God Jar. I have used this also. With a God Jar, I wrote my desires on strips of paper and put them in the jar and left them alone. It was wonderful in those years when I was still building my belief to see at the end of the year when I opened the jar and read through them all that had come into my life that I desired and may have even forgotten I had asked for. I was also able to see that many of the things that happened during that time that I perceived as difficult and challenging and even painful were all a part of helping me to become a match to my desire so it could reach me.

You are combining the two main tools I have given you. You are creating a vision of the life you want to live, and you are writing down all the desires that you are aware of that are a part of that complete vision and life.

At first, I tell you to spend five minutes with each of these tools every day for thirty days. When you begin working with these tools and actively creating the life you want to live, you are learning so much, becoming aware of so many things, and applying new ideas, perspectives, techniques, and tools to help you. My desire is for you to move to a place with my help in teaching you this where it becomes a way of living and being rather than just tools you use. You can learn to live in this more than not, and things will come to you with so much more grace and ease.

Right now, give yourself grace as you learn, grow, and evolve. This is the work, and it will work on you. As you move through that, it will work for you.

CHAPTER 7

Are You Committed to Finding Your Freedom?

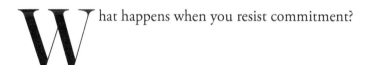 hat happens when you resist commitment?

> *There's a difference between interest and commitment.*
> *When you're interested in doing something, you do it only*
> *when circumstances permit. When you're committed to*
> *something, you accept no excuses, only results.*
> —Ken Blanchard

I still remember the day over a decade ago, sitting in San Diego in a conference aimed at getting me in touch with and connected to my big mission and my big life, and the woman on stage looking right at me, asked, "Are you merely interested or committed?"

Wow! What a question. That one not only spoke to me; it reached out and grabbed me by the shoulders and shook me a little. Up until that moment, I had been dabbling, playing in the possibilities, dreaming about all the things I could do and would do. I had big intentions. And yet, I was dancing around the edges, dipping my toe in, surveying the surface, without diving in.

She called me to action that day, and nothing has ever been the same since. Everything I had learned and experienced up to that moment had prepared me to step into the fullness of it. All I had to do was show up, just as I was.

Randy Pausch, who is well-known for his speech "The Last Lecture," said, "The brick walls are there for a reason. The brick walls are not there to keep us out; the brick walls are there to give us a chance to show how badly we want something. The brick walls are there to stop the people who don't want it badly enough. They are there to stop the other people!"

It's when you come to that place, your own brick wall, that you make a choice to either commit or retreat. You are always either moving towards or away from your goal, your vision, your mission, your truth. In that moment lies the opportunity to say, "I am doing this!," to face what is in your way, open up to the next step and move forward, doing what is necessary to create the future you are meant to be living now.

When you retreat, nothing happens. At first. But when you have a big vision, a mission calling to you, a purpose for being here on this planet that you are not expressing, and dreams for something better, it will eat away at you slowly. You will become more and more disconnected from your truth, from who you really are, and from your Source that feeds and supports you into your greatness.

I lived in this desert for a long time. Many years. I wandered in a wilderness of my own making. I cried out. I got stuck. I lost touch with myself, forgot my greatness. I found a million reasons why I could not, would not, should not pursue my purpose on this planet right then. I made promises to myself that I did not keep. It ate me alive from the inside out.

Something very important is always hiding just behind your resistance to making a commitment to yourself to step into who you are and take that out into the world. It's both the prison and the key to your freedom. Your choice in every moment defines it.

The moment you commit to yourself and to that greater something, everything changes. Your perspective changes. Instead of making excuses, you seek results.

It is said that, "Until one is committed, there is hesitancy, the chance to draw back, always ineffectiveness. Concerning all acts of initiative (and creation), there is one elementary truth, the ignorance of which kills countless ideas and splendid plans: that the moment one definitely commits oneself, then Providence moves, too. All sorts of things occur to help one that would never otherwise have occurred. A whole stream of events issues from the decision, raising in one's favor all manner of unforeseen incidents and meetings and material assistance, which no man could have dreamed would have come his way." (J. W. von Goethe)

This is precisely where the magic happens!

You must sound the call, engage first, and set in motion all that is ready to rush in to be a part of your creation and your bigger life, once you are ready for it.

I have had a lot of clients come to me playing the when/then game. They give me a list of what they want and tell me they will do everything I recommend to them if I can guarantee they will get what they want from doing it. At the same time, they tell their Trusted Source, "When you provide me with all of this, then I will answer the call."

That's not how it works. We came here for the experience. A perfect plan does not pre-exist; it becomes as we grow and evolve. It's an organic process, and it's miraculous.

Do you want it badly enough?

Are you merely interested or committed?

A powerful coach once posted on Facebook, "Is your coach confronting you and creating consequences? They should be."

My answer was no, so I hired her.

What we resist, persists. You can make excuses, or you can seek results. Where I go deeper is to help you understand that your "excuses" are so much more complex than "Just do it," and that you can clear, heal, and resolve them to find your Freedom.

When I first started becoming aware of my true desires and the strong urge to create a life I loved instead of living my life by default, I discovered the desire to be who I am and do what I am here to do, not just what I can do, and to be all of who I am. This led me to make a life-altering decision to get rid of my license as a therapist and open my own Healing Center in the community I had just moved into. At the time, this felt super scary, risky, maybe not responsible, illogical, inconvenient, and potentially expensive. I have come to learn that if it feels really exciting and really scary at the same time, those are the things I must do.

I had two of my three children still at home and college to start preparing for, and we had just made a big move, with my husband starting a new job. I went against my knowing at first, and I took a job that I felt right there in my solar plexus was not the right thing for me to do as I was on the phone accepting it. Shortly after that, I was released from that job in a very sudden and unexpected way, and I got the message. It's time, and you have been ASKING.

I tell my clients this all the time. If you are asking for what you desire, and you don't take inspired, aligned action toward what you are asking for, the Universe still has to deliver it to you. And that can look like a mess. When you see someone where it appears that the rug has been pulled out from under them, this is what is going on. Maybe you've experienced this yourself? The things that come easiest to you are those where you have high desire and low resistance. The things that create upset in your life are those where you have high desire and high resistance. I go so far as to tell my clients who are not going to take action on what they are asking for to stop asking, stop desiring. However, those upsets can be the greatest gifts.

I was devastated when I was let go from that job. My head was spinning, because none of it made sense. I had never been let go from a job in my life, and the reason for this was perplexing and confusing. It was Christmastime, we were in a new home in a new city and state, and we had so much disruption around us.

That was the last job I have ever had, by the way. I have not been employed by anyone else since 2006. I started my business in 2007 and have put into practice all that I am teaching you. My life has been profoundly changed in all the best ways over the past sixteen years. I am unrecognizable from who I was even a decade ago and more so two decades ago. It has stretched me and grown me. The payoff is absolutely worth it. It gets better and better.

My next desire for Freedom was for Money Freedom. I had a mentor who showed me that financial freedom is not how much money you have in the bank. Financial freedom is knowing how to create the money you need and want when you need and want it. This path required me to get right with my money and Money, in general. Money is a great spiritual teacher.

I found that building my own business was the most intensive personal and spiritual growth program I could ever enroll in. I had to develop the mindset to make it happen alongside the strategic skills and knowledge to make it work. And I applied all that I was learning to all areas of my life. One thing you will find about me the more we journey together is that I never ask you to do anything I haven't done. I always go first, and I turn around and reach for your hand and show you the way once I am on the other side of it. I will share with you everything I learned and tell you all about my journey.

My Money Journey was a long and bumpy road. I had a lot of support and guidance along the way. I stayed the course. I stayed in the room. I did the inner work that was required of me. And it serves me well every day of my life now. I broke through all those walls I bumped up against, and when I turned around, every one of them was no longer there. They had disappeared, because they were an illusion created by me.

A few years ago, we manifested a desire of mine to retire my husband from his life-time career in public education. I wanted to get off living according to a school calendar, and I wanted him to be able to travel with me. Over the past few years, building my business, I created the travel experiences I had always desired. I was able to travel all over the world, combining work and pleasure and family and friend time. I was ready for him to be able to go with me.

I became aware of my desire for Time Freedom. I love my work, and I have always worked a lot. My work is part of my life, and I have created a very integrated life. The living of my life is my work. In 2020, my business boomed as many people in need showed up to work with me and to connect with each other. I worked more in 2020 and 2021 and carried more clients and students than I ever had before. Then, we retired my husband, and we became grandparents for the first time. Our second grandbaby came to us very recently. Now, I wanted Time Freedom, and it was a new desire for me.

I talk to you about how your desires would change, and new desires would bubble up and show themselves to you. You may see suddenly where what you thought you desired you no longer do, and the direction you thought you wanted to go in is changing to create your current desires. Even a few years ago, I was working a lot and loving every minute of it. I could not imagine it being any other way. I would hear people talking about retiring, and I would be asked, when am I going to retire, and it was not even on my radar. Then a new desire started showing up, and as I felt into it, and as I honored it, new and wonderful things began showing up in my life and for me and my family.

In the process, some things showed up that I had to let go of. I was taking action, assessing, adjusting, and course correcting as I am teaching you to. I was reading the feedback, following the breadcrumbs, and responding to the opportunities that were showing up. Some of them were very big, very exciting, somewhat scary, seemed illogical, involved doing things that were inconvenient, and came with costs that felt expensive. But I know better!

One gift out of this is the ability now with a portion of the time that opened up for me to put my time, energy, and resources into a passion project close to my heart that I have been aware of and that needed me now. It showed up, not a part of my now plan, but calling me, and I was able to go all in. As I am a blessing here, I have been so fully blessed.

When you learn to trust your desires, to follow your pleasure rather than use pain as a motivator, and take aligned inspired action toward what you want, time often collapses, and things come into your life, ready for you, much sooner than you expected. This has happened to me many times. We have experienced timelines shortening by years. It's all possible, and once you become a match to it, it's yours now. The joy that is created by the manifestation of a desire brings more desires to you, desires you have had out there for years. I call it riding the wave, and I love to see how long I can stay in this wave of energy and how much good I am willing to receive.

I had some coaches over the years ask me, "How much good are you willing to receive?" It's a powerful question, and it's an important question.

It's very human of us to put self-imposed limits on how much good we will allow ourselves to receive. We worry about what other people think. We operate from misguided programming and conditioning that has told us we can't or shouldn't. We hold untrue beliefs that us having more will cause someone else to have less. This is one of the most crippling beliefs and widely spread.

You having more will never cause anyone else to have less. We each have our own pie. What you don't receive of your own pie is lost to you. It is not for anyone else. Each person creates their life experience with their whole pie through their choice points in every moment. How often have you not taken all you desire for fear that someone else will think you are greedy, call you selfish, or not have enough themselves?

It is not noble to suffer. That is an outdated notion perpetuated by those in power, primarily the Church, to keep control over the people and their possessions.

One of the greatest gifts I ever received from a coach of mine was when she told me, The Highest Good of All has to include you or it's not the Highest Good. When she first said it, my mind could not accept it. I struggled with it and resisted the idea of it. Now, I cannot imagine anything else being true except this, and I live it. The Highest Good of All has to include you or it's not the Highest Good. To take that further, I have learned that when I am about my Highest Good and operate from this place, everyone else in my world is better for it. That doesn't mean some won't kick up some backlash along the way. Remember, other people are very invested in you staying the same, but that's their agenda, not yours.

I will go so far now as to say, The Highest Good of All has to be for your Highest Good first and foremost, but . . . baby steps . . . I will leave that for later.

I will ask you now, How much good are you willing to receive?

CHAPTER 8

Are You Motivated
to Master Your Manifesting?

O nce a colleague and friend of mine asked me, this work you do with others and have done in your own life, can you teach it to me? At the time, I was doing this work, testing it out and finding my way. I always go first. I walk through the fires. Then, I turn around and share them with you. In 2003, I turned my life into an experiment with the Law of Attraction, and that grew into my business and my life. So, I had been doing these things, but I was not yet teaching them.

Her question got me thinking, because my answer to her was no. I wasn't sure what I was doing or how. I was still practicing and mastering my craft, putting in my 10,000 hours, and still in the early stages of that.

This exploration of what I was doing and the results I was getting led me to put it into words for the first time. I went through an interesting exercise to discover the process I was using in working with my clients and the results I was getting.

I realized that my work would move forward into new expressions when I could teach others what I was doing to get the results I was getting. And, so, this 5 Steps to Mastery and Manifestation was born.

This is my Unique System, the way I work with my clients and students and the way I first transformed my own life. Here is the foundation for my work.

DISCOVER: Begin creating awareness. Whatever you are ready to work on and release will show up. Learn to work with the unconscious, subconscious, and conscious to bring to the surface what no longer serves you so that you can shift it and move forward, out of what you don't want and into what you do want.

SHIFT: Clear, heal, and resolve what is getting in your way. If it is showing up in your world, you have called it forth into consciousness so you can release it. There are many ways to do this. It is far-reaching and will create powerful change in yourself and your life. At any given time, you have a variety of life situations you are experiencing. They may not always at first appear to be related, or you are so close to them that you cannot see what is really going on. These life situations are symptoms, and they can lead you directly to the root causes and the underlying energetic situations you are playing out at your deepest level. When you make changes at this level, these things stop showing up. They are showing up for you to clear, heal and resolve, and they are coming to the surface now, because you are asking for things, you are setting intentions and radiating desire. These things that are showing up are in response to that. This is what is showing up that no longer serves you, that you cannot take with you where you want to go, that you cannot hold onto as who you want to be, and that will not be able to exist alongside what you want to have. All of this holds valuable feedback and resources so you can get to the root cause, stop the symptomatology that is the repeating life situations showing up in their varied forms, and get to the core of what is really going on, so you can consciously create change for the better.

ACT: Your next step is the one that most people get stuck at, and many do not move forward at this point, often for many, many years, sometimes for a lifetime. You must take new action to get new results. Learn to read the feedback, do your work in the physical third-dimensional world, and allow Universal Energy to work with you and for you. Working with the Divine Intelligence and The Field works in the Fifth Dimension. The Fourth Dimension is where we work with our thoughts and feelings. When we stop here, we create a rich inner world that is not reflected in our outer world. We long to escape more and more into this world. Our physical world continues to deteriorate. At some point, we begin to lose the ability to create what we need to meet our basic needs. We are left longing for love, money, relationships, fulfilling work, a home that is our sanctuary, and other worldly things that continue to elude us.

BELIEVE: As we take new action, we are able to build new beliefs, to find and integrate new evidence to support these beliefs, to get rid of limiting beliefs and to anchor in new desirable beliefs that support us very powerfully in manifesting what we desire. We first must do the emotional work of clearing, healing, and resolving. Much of this has been overlaid upon who we truly authentically are throughout our life and beginning in utero. This is the stuff that keeps us stuck. We have pushed much of it deep into our unconscious and subconscious, but it is still driving our bus. From here, we can move forward to do the mindset work.

We act on what we believe, not what we know.

CREATE: Now, you step fully into being the Creator of your own experience. You move away from Victim energy and the perpetual cycle of Victim/Rescuer/Victim and into the powerful cycle of Creator. With more responsibility comes more power. And it is always your choice. Create what you want. Live the life you desire and dream of.

These are the 5 stages, the natural progression you move through to come to this place of PERSONAL POWER and DIVINE ABUNDANCE.

We must become the Master before we can Manifest. Learn to:

- Master your Self
- Master your Emotions
- Master your Energy
- Master your Gifts
- Master your Mindset

The truth is you can't get what you want by just thinking happy thoughts about it. You have to take action. That is the real secret. It's the key to everything. I want you to get this; action is not how we create what we desire, it is how we receive what is already there for us. We have to take third-dimensional real-world action to bring what we desire into third-dimensional form.

TAKE INSPIRED ACTION Tool

Here is how it works to make it easy for you as you're learning something new and putting it into practice. I've broken it down into a simple exercise with four steps.

Take out a blank index card. I love working with index cards. You can use a piece of paper or your journal. But I like teaching this with an index card, and I use them a lot.

1. Set an intention of something you want to create. Write it down on an index card. Be very clear. Be very specific. The important thing is to stay with what you want without regard to how it could happen. Write it in the present. I am, I have, I am doing . . . Universal Principle: leave the how's to the Universe. This is an important Universal Law that will absolutely determine your results. Set an intention in the present of something you are being, doing, or having. Set an intention of something you want to create, and write it down on the note card.

2. Come up with new actions you're willing to take to make this happen. Write them down on the other side of the note card. Flip it over. This is not about springing into action and just doing, doing, doing. This is about getting into a quiet, reflective place and connecting with what you want and writing it down. Write what comes to you. This is not an exercise for your mind. This is for you to see what is there and bring it forward. If you hear it, feel it, sense it, see a vision of it, or know it, write it down. Become inspired and write down actions you're inspired to take, things that seem to come in out of left field. Ask and it is given is a

Universal Principle. It is found in every sacred text, and it is absolutely true. When you ask, the Universe always begins delivering to you what you are asking for.

Most people just aren't prepared for how it actually shows up in comparison to how they expect it to show up. When you ask, begin immediately to watch for opportunities to show up, and remember this; they will not be logical, comfortable, or convenient. They will stretch and grow you. If you didn't need to stretch and grow to receive them, you would already have them.

They're not going to be comfortable. They're not going to be convenient; they're going to appear illogical, and sometimes they seem expensive.

3. Follow through with at least one. Circle one of the actions you have written on the index card that you are willing to do now. Get into inspired aligned action right away.

I thought I was good and quick about getting into inspired aligned action. I had to learn to do it even better. Right away, bring it onto the 3D plane, bring it into form. Take one action, then watch for feedback. Stay in action. Learn to Act, Assess, and Adjust. Course correct as needed.

Just don't stop. The Universe will continue to give you feedback. Watch for breadcrumbs, and follow the breadcrumbs, especially when they don't make sense. Just follow the breadcrumbs.

4. Make it happen, and watch the Universe go to work for you. The Universe responds to true need. It does not play

the when/then game. You always have to take the first step, then it will rush in to meet you. You're building a trust muscle here. Trust x 3. Trust Yourself. Trust Divine Intelligence. Trust the Process.

Try this first with small things, less important things. Don't try this right away with things that trigger you emotionally. The easiest things to manifest are those which you have a high desire for and low resistance to.

Hang on to the card. Hang it up where you can see it. Track your progress on it.

This works best when you can stay engaged but detached from the outcome. That's another one you're most likely going to need to work on. You can affirm and write on the card, "Thank you for this or something better." Leave the door open for something to show up that is better than what you were asking for.

This is key. I do this all the time. Then, when what I desired or asked for doesn't show up, I'm certain it's because there's something better, and it happens every single time that I don't start telling stories that create what I don't want. Most of the time what I want shows up. Every time the "something better" showed up, I was able to see the Divine orchestration behind it, and it was.

You can't even imagine the miracles the Universe can deliver to you. When it shows up, express gratitude, and amplify it. Pat yourself on the back, celebrate, put the card up on your celebration board, or tuck it into your gratitude journal, and then go for the next one.

At first, these are things you do. They're things you're doing, they're new ways of thinking, new patterns of behavior, and new ways of doing things. Your brain has to get used to them, your physiology, your body, and, over time, they become more than things you do. They become a way of living and a way of being right before your eyes.

A Word About Naysayers

When people undermine your dreams, predict your doom, or criticize you, remember, they're telling you their story, not yours.
—Cynthia Occelli

This was shared with me early on, and it has helped me so many times.

It's actually a psychological process that's going on, and it's pretty predictable.

I had a new client just the other day who finally decided to do this, and her stuff was kicking up all week long: what will people think, what will people say? She was programmed and conditioned with, what will the neighbors think? What will people think? What will people say? You've got to be proper and right, and you've got to stay in the tribe, stay in the community, stay in the society, stay in the culture. And, don't bring shame to it.

It can be difficult to break through those things. The more she talked about it, the more I could see the inner work that was going to have to happen for her to really break through to those goals she had set and the results she desires. She had been putting off and putting off what she truly desired, what she wanted, and what she needed. This had been going on for a very long time, running the show. This is why this inner work is so integral and so powerful.

I love the story one of my coaches told me, and it has really stuck with me. In fact, I use it as an example for where people are stuck, because so many can identify with it. I observed this all the time with people in my community and with my clients and students.

"Have you ever watched crabs in a bucket?" she asked me.

The bucket does not have a tarp on it, and yet the crabs are not able to escape.

Now, if there is only one crab in the bucket, it can and will escape easily. However, when there are many crabs in the bucket, as soon as one crab tries to escape by climbing out, the other crabs will grab hold of it and pull it back down into the bucket to share the mutual fate of the rest of the group. Really get this, this is an example of nature that can be translated into human nature. It is wired into us as humans in our DNA in our earliest times generationally, and in the human experience.

There was a time when we could not survive outside of the tribe that we were born into or brought into. It is inside of you, this impulse. Stay with the tribe, stay within the norms of the tribe, be like the tribe. Yet, there were always trailblazers and naysayers and risk takers, and that's how so much forward movement happened despite this, that's how humans have grown and developed over time. But, this is still in us, and it can kick up in you.

This whole thing about not being able to survive without the tribe runs deep, but now you can go out and you can create your own tribes. Maybe you are meant to be a leader of a new tribe or find new people to connect with.

Are you aware of a time, in the past or right now, where you tried to climb up and look over the side of that bucket, and the other crabs pulled you back down? As you begin to get the urge for a fuller experience of life and a fuller expression of yourself, when you respond to the calling and make the choice to step onto this path to take the first step of the journey, it's going to be necessary to climb out of the crab bucket.

> *We evolve at the rate of the tribe we are plugged into.*
> —Caroline Myss

Often, you find there are those who are not there to support you. Do not waste time and energy trying to figure it out, because, across the board, some of the people you think will be there for you will not, and some of the people you think would be a problem and not be for you or about it can surprise you in a positive way.

Keep Calm, Heal Your Crap, and Carry On!

It takes support and guidance to climb out of the crab bucket, to make a choice and commitment to yourself to be a conscious creator of your own life and experience. Perhaps you've been very well socialized to live a "normal life." Yet, something is calling you to be more, do more, and have more. It may have been calling you for a very long time, or you shut it out, and then it comes back.

The standards being set in our world today often speak to the path of mediocrity. Play it safe, live by this set of rules, norms, and expectations, and you will get by. This way of living limits your growth, the reaching of your highest potential, and the creation of your best life. It limits your greatness. Those who respond to the calling of their Higher Self toward all they desire discover something. They discover their authentic self and a more rewarding life.

They take action to create a life they love, the life of their dreams. They're not going to be pulled back down into that crab bucket one more time. As you move into higher consciousness, connecting with your Truth becomes a stronger call. When you are in alignment with your Truth and begin to spend more of your time and energy consciously creating, your life flows.

You begin to attract to you everything you need. Things begin to come together more easily and effortlessly. Call it synchronicity, call it miracles. Move out of pain and frustration, out of feeling trapped or stuck, out of a life that no longer serves you and feels like it no longer fits.

M.O.V.E. into the life you desire.

So, you climb out of the crab bucket, what's next? How do you get your dreams out of your head and into the world?

Grab an index card, and do the exercise.

Then, let's get M.O.V.E.'ing forward!

PART TWO

The Plan

CHAPTER 9

Are You Set to M.O.V.E.?

An Assessment for You: HOW DO YOU KNOW WHEN YOU ARE READY FOR A BREAKTHROUGH? It's amazing what kind of TRANSFORMATION you are capable of creating in your life when you make a decision and are committed to having a breakthrough. It's your Intention that carries the initial power that starts moving you forward and causes all the unseen forces that start conspiring on your behalf for your Highest Good.

Here are some telltale signs.

You are ready for a breakthrough if YOU ARE:

- Really wanting to make changes in your life and ready to move in this direction
- Transitioning out of what no longer serves you
- Ready to embrace your purpose
- Passionate about your vision, your mission, your dreams, your truth

- A person that others naturally turn to for guidance or you want to be
- Tired of losing yourself in everyone and everything else
- So done with giving yourself away
- No longer willing to be an energy source for others in a way that drains the life out of you
- Wanting to stop constantly shifting your energy to accommodate others
- Willing to step out of living out stories that no longer serve you
- Ready to honor your true self
- Ready to stand for yourself
- Preparing to stand for those you are here to serve
- Ready to make heart-centered intuitive decisions
- Ready to own your own agenda and create a life you love
- Ready to step into the spotlight of your own life
- Seeking to master your two greatest and most powerful tools— your energy and your intuition—to transform your life
- Stepping up to ask for what you want, become a match, and attract it
- Looking to experience relief and freedom that brings a new joy to your life
- Seeking the possibilities for yourself
- Committed to stepping into your greatness
- Open to going to the next level in your life

You are ready for a breakthrough if YOUR CURRENT STRUGGLES INCLUDE:

- Not knowing where to start

- Wanting control over your energy and your life
- Experiencing stress and fear that comes with stepping into your brilliance and your vision, your mission, your dreams and your truth
- Recognizing that a lot of energy is going out, but not a lot is coming in for you
- Losing your confidence due to criticism or weak support
- Questioning, "Can I really make this change?" "Can I really do this?"
- Spending lots of time being busy but feeling you don't have what you want to show for it
- Spinning your wheels, stuck in old patterns, falling back into what is comfortable and safe but not necessarily good for you
- Continually losing momentum and having to get started again
- Feeling isolated and alone
- Unfocused
- Lacking clarity
- Overwhelmed, shut down
- Unclear about how to move forward in any area of your life
- Coming up with lots of great ideas but not sure at all how to get started implementing them
- Finding yourself frustrated with inconsistent action and inconsistent results
- Feeling you have no time for yourself or not enough time for yourself to live the life you want to live
- You're tired
- Your stress level is high

- You can't see a way out of living the way you are living, but you know it's no longer working for you
- You are exhausted and close to burning out
- You've outgrown your current life or parts of it
- You want something more
- You know it's time to step fully into your life purpose, but you aren't sure how
- Wanting to stop struggling but you don't feel you can do it on your own
- Really ready to take a quantum leap in at least one area of your life rather than just creeping along but you lack the guidance, support and accountability that will assure your success

You are ready for a breakthrough if YOU FEEL THE NEED TO:

- Make a plan
- Move forward into action
- Learn to manage your Energy
- Reconnect with your Intuition, that part of you that knows what you really want, what you desire and intend, and also knows how to get you there
- Learn to create consistent results
- Create a lifestyle that supports you
- Integrate a rich spiritual life that you are longing to live into a successful physical life
- Make changes in what you are doing and how you are doing it

- Shift your models
- Experience a Mindset Makeover
- Bust Limiting Beliefs and Build New Beliefs
- Work Smarter, Not Harder
- Up-level your energy and enthusiasm to support your vision, your mission, your dreams and your truth
- Create a fresh new start
- Get the support and guidance you need
- Plug into a high-energy community and tribe of your own
- Be supported in initiating a major up-leveling and mindset shift so exponential growth can happen with ease
- Take control over your own life and time

I believe, personal transformation is an integral part of societal and global transformation and all true change is dependent on and supported by those who are willing to transform at a personal level and then lead others to do the same.

I am so passionate about this as the way to create true beneficial and sustainable transformation, to change your world and the world in the process, that I wrote my dissertation on this to receive my Doctorate in Transformational Spiritual Coaching, and I have dedicated my life and my work to it.

You know you are ready for a breakthrough. Now, it's time to make a decision.

After living the first few years of building and growing my business and myself, someone asked me, can you teach someone how to do what you are doing? That really gave me pause to think. I needed to not only be doing this powerful life-changing and game-changing work, but I needed to start intentionally being able to put words to it, so that I could teach others how to do it for themselves and for those they are called to serve.

At the time I was writing my first book and developing my first signature talk, and getting up on the stage for the first time other than some local speaking gigs I had gotten along the way, I developed this acronym and this simple formula to help you understand how you can move forward in any area of your life.

M.O.V.E.

Before I go any further with this, you can go to www.Intuitive-SuccessCoach.com and get my free 21-Day Email Course that will guide you through this in real time. Give me fifteen or twenty minutes a day for twenty-one days, and watch what happens. I can teach you about this, but guiding and supporting you through the actual process can be so much more beneficial.

The *M* is the first step in the formula: **Make A Decision.**

It all begins with a decision. And, understand this, a decision has not been made until an action has been taken. But there are a few steps in between, and they are very important. You don't need to make a bunch of decisions. You only need to make one, right now, in this moment. When you make this decision and commit to it, then take aligned inspired action, energetic shifts will occur to line you up with the opportunities to move you forward and then to the next decision. Too often, people come to me, and they want to jump ahead steps and know things they think they need to know that they don't need to know and that will just use up precious vital life force energy and scatter their focus when they don't yet need it. That kept me from writing my first book for four years!

The *O* is the second step in the formula. **Own It 100 percent.**

This is a crucial piece of this puzzle. Once you make a decision, you need to own it 100 percent. This means, you need to cut out all the second guessing and self-doubting, the one foot in and one foot out, the wavering, the wobbling . . . and, you need to protect this energy from the input of others. You will have enough going on working to keep your limiting beliefs and programming and conditioning from crashing the whole effort at this point.

This is where Energy Management and Emotional Mastery come in. This is something I talk about all the time and a big part of the work I have been doing alongside building and growing my business over the past sixteen years.

In yoga, there is a pose called the Mountain Pose. In Mountain Pose, you stand with your feet hip distance apart. You really feel your feet, lift and spread the toes and get a firm connection with the ground beneath you. Stand tall, spine tall and straight, strong arms to your sides, fingers pointing down. This is an energetic stance of strength and balance. This pose is a physical embodiment of standing strong like a mountain.

In the same way, imagine you are in a strong wind whipping at you from all sides. Are you the beach ball being batted around by the wind, or the energies of others, or are you the tree, standing strong, roots firmly planted, bending but not breaking?

At first, you may only be able to own this decision and support yourself 100 percent for short periods of time. This is for you to work on, and it will serve you greatly.

TOOL: The *V* is the third step in the formula. **Visualize It.**

This is a tool for you to develop and use. I tell my clients and students, use this tool for just five minutes a day for thirty days, and watch what happens.

Spend five minutes a day in your Vision. At first, you will be "imagining" it and creating it. What does it look like? What does it feel like? What do you see? Where are you living? What are you doing each day? What are you driving? Who is around you? What are you eating? What are you doing with your free time? How do you feel? What are you thinking? What are you saying?

As you work within your Vision, it will begin to take on an energy of its own. Things will begin to show up that might surprise you or spark something within you. Things will begin to show up in your outer world in response to what you are experiencing in your Vision.

The *E* is the fourth step in the formula. **Execute It.**

You have Made a Decision.

You Own it 100 percent.

You are Visualizing it.

Now is the time to Take Action.

This is not just any action; this is Aligned Inspired Action. This is not just doing, doing, doing, busy, busy, busy. This is Taking Action from an inspired and empowered place.

Remember earlier when we talked about information coming to you through Inspiration or Data? Now you can see how important and integral this is to the process.

Picture this. You're on the set. Everything has been staged just as you imagined. All the players have shown up and been given their roles. Now, that moment, a pause, as all energies come together into a very clear focus. You are leaning into it.

The director shouts, Ready! Set! Action!

What gets everything and everyone in motion? Action!

Action is the lynchpin of the whole manifestation process. Nothing happens without it.

Oh, yeah, you might experience the good feelings. There's a high that comes from visualizing and dreaming. But your results remain in your head and are expressed through your thoughts and feelings. It is not until you take action that things show up here in your physical world.

I always say, do the energetic work first! It saves so much time. But don't stop there. You still have to take action.

I have made a living and created a successful business the past decade out of helping people **master the art of taking inspired action**. Why? Because people get stuck just before this step. They get frozen, feel paralyzed. And, so, they do nothing. And then they get nothing. A year goes by, and they are still in the same place they were 365 days before. They still have what they've always had, but it's painful, because they still have the dreams and desires for something more. Those didn't go away.

Haven't you been getting ready and set long enough? Isn't it time to dive in? There has never been a better time than now. There never will be.

What I discovered was that it's really easier than I thought. Much of it was in my mind. Once I got into action, I found that if I just stayed in action, I could take baby steps, and I could create profound results. And I have been doing that now specifically and consistently for years, and it has made all the difference in my world.

You are always, ALWAYS, either moving towards or away from your goal, your vision, your mission, your truth, and the life of your dreams. In every moment, there is a choice point to get into action or to retreat. Do not fool yourself into thinking that standing still will not have an impact. There is no true still. In every moment, you are making choices that are either moving you towards or away from what you want and where you want to be. Not taking action IS an action.

You have a choice point in every moment. Every decision you make and action you take either moves you toward or away from what you want. This is where you get really honest with yourself. And own it 100 percent.

It's time to stop talking and start walking in the direction of your dreams and desires.

How much time and energy have you spent talking about what you want to do? And what are you doing about it?

If you're being honest with yourself, it sounds like you need to learn to master the art of taking action and M.O.V.E. into Aligned Inspired Action.

So many people around you are talking about what they're going to do, but, really, is anything actually happening? Talk is cheap. It's what you do that counts.

Remember, a decision has not been made until an action has been taken. That is what gets your dream out of your head and into the world. That is what brings you real world third-dimensional results in answer to what you need, want, and desire.

Now, let's get M.O.V.E.'ing!

While we're talking about Transforming Beliefs, I want to share with you this article I wrote:

LIONS AND TIGERS AND BELIEFS, OH MY!
by Dr. Michelle Barr

Every day, in the work I do, I come across beliefs that have taken root in people and are keeping them from moving forward, creating what they desire, and maintaining their successes.

These beliefs are driving your bus, and yet, much of the time you are not even aware of them. At some point, they became a part of you. Now, they are holding you back.

Identifying and letting go of beliefs that no longer serve you is at the heart of transformation work.

It begins with a belief you have accepted, usually very early in your life, and it has become fact. Your subconscious uses this belief to navigate you through your daily life, and you are nudged to notice everything that is in line with and supports this belief. Thus, you get what you expect.

I have seen miracles occur as soon as a belief is loosened and dissolved and replaced with a more powerful and supportive belief. Reality is restructured. Life begins to be very different.

Affirmations were all the craze years ago. Positive thought. And yet, people continue to show up and tell me, "I am saying all these affirmations, and they are not working." You can't fool the body. And the Universe does not listen to your words. It responds to your emotions—your energy in motion.

You have to:

- Get in touch with the belief
- Determine the strength of the belief
- Connect with the feelings around the belief
- Crack through the resistance the limiting belief is creating
- Build a new belief

Recently, I was doing a session with a client. This was our second session together, and we dove deep into a limiting belief that had stopped her for twenty-four years.

Imagine shifting a belief that has a hold on you like that and beginning to create more good in your life.

Pick a belief, any belief, and get started bringing it to the surface, so you can deal with it head on. And pretty soon, "Toto, I've a feeling we're not in Kansas anymore!"

All it takes is a little courage.

It's within your reach. As Dorothy says, "If I ever go looking for my heart's desire again, I won't look any further than my own backyard." It begins right within, in your own "backyard."

CHAPTER 10

Are You Asking the Right Questions?

T he process of transforming your dreams into your everyday reality begins by examining some of the pitfalls. One of these is the questions you are asking.

Remember, your thoughts have power. Your feelings have energy. Your emotions are energy in motion. And they all affect the action you will take or not take.

Ask the Right Questions.

When you want to ask, "Why is this happening to me?" ask, instead, "What have I been asking for?" The two questions are worlds apart and create very different energies in your body.

When you are asking, "Why? Why is this happening to me? What did I do?," you are folding into yourself, constricting your energy, closing yourself off, and putting yourself into a helpless and hopeless victim stance.

When you ask, "What have I been asking for?," you open to answers, you expand your energy and access Divine Intelligence and inner wisdom.

I swear by this. I have worked with thousands of clients at this point, and whenever things start showing up in their life that they don't want, they don't like, and that bring them pain and discomfort, I always ask them, "Tell me what you have been asking for."

What powerful intentions have they been setting, either consciously or unconsciously?

I am always able to find a connection between what is showing up that they don't want along with or instead of what they want and what they have been asking for. What shows up that is a match to what you are asking for shows you where you are already a match to what you need, want, and desire. It shows you where you are already open to receive and allow what you are asking for and intending. What shows up that you don't want is there to show you what needs to be cleared, healed, and resolved so that you can receive and allow what you are asking for and intending. It's all feedback, and when you learn how to use it as a tool for transformation, it gives you so much creative power.

When something happens to you that throws you off course or doesn't fit into your plans, you often begin to question.

"Why is this happening to me?"

"What did I do to deserve this?"

"What am I going to do about this?"

The better question to ask would be, "What have I been asking for?"

You see, nothing happens by coincidence. Nothing comes to you without reason. Anything that shows up in your world can only come to you because, in some way, it matches what you are asking for.

You get to ask for whatever you want, and you send that out into the Universe through your feelings and desires. Sometimes, you are using tools that are helping you to consciously create your circumstances, as well. At any time, there exists a continuum, and you are both consciously creating and unconsciously creating.

What you don't orchestrate is the how of it all, and this is where building trust with the All That Is really serves you. Always, there is a bigger picture. You are a part of it, along with everyone and everything else. You ask for what you want, and then the Universe goes to work to deliver it.

Now, here's where things get messy. Many times, I have asked for things in my life, and then when they come about, I am surprised. I mean, I would NEVER orchestrate things to happen that way. That's not the way I envisioned this would go. Yet, as it all unfolds, I do see that what I want is what is coming to me, or trying to, at least. A Higher Wisdom is at work here and a Higher Intelligence.

In this same way, I have had times when I have told Divine Intelligence exactly what I want and left the how's completely up to Universal Design.

Years ago, I started letting Divine Intelligence know what I wanted in my life. I really felt it, and I got specific . . . in the essence of it. I said, I don't know how any of this can or will happen. It's what I want, though. And I went on about my business.

While I was doing what I am here to do, getting up every morning and stepping out into the world, offering what I have, creating value, and being in inspired action, engaged in the cycle of giving and receiving, the Universe began delivering all these incredible things and circumstances to me in ways that I could not have ever dreamed up. I sit here today having made huge life changes that bring me immense joy and satisfaction and support the work I am doing in the world and the life I want to live with my husband and my children, my family and friends, and my community.

And it has been the easiest and most effortless thing to receive. Ever.

I mean, I KNOW this stuff works. I teach it. I coach people through it. It's a way of living for me now. But still, from time to time, I get surprised by the impeccable way this all works.

The Law of Attraction works. It's on all the time. You don't choose to engage with it, do a little manifesting, then turn it off and go back into your toxic relationships, environments, thoughts, habits, and patterns.

It all counts. It all matters.

When people come to me in crisis, the first thing I do is have them go back and look at the intentions they have been setting recently and what they have been asking for. Almost immediately, I am able to help them identify patterns and relationships so they see why the things in their life are showing up the way they are. It is always on target.

"Why is this happening to me?" creates a constrictive energy. You turn in on yourself. You feel victimized. You close yourself off. You shut down.

"What have I been asking for?" creates an expansive energy that you can work with to move forward. You are not a victim. Instead, you are a Powerful Creator. You are receiving feedback from the Universe, and there is great benefit for you here. What is showing up now is bringing you what you have been asking for. Here is hope. Here is promise. This shift in energy alone lifts you up out of a stagnant space so you can grow.

Many times, what is showing up first is what you need to clear, heal, and resolve so that you can receive what you have been asking for.

Yes, it will stretch and grow you. If you were already a match to it, you would already have it.

Try this the next time something shows up that doesn't feel good to you or seems at first glance to be counterproductive to what you are dreaming about and desiring. Examine where your trust lies, in yourself and in your connection to the All That Is.

Then ask yourself, "What have I been asking for?" Open to the answers. They might surprise you.

CHAPTER 11

Are You Setting Goals and Intentions?

W hether you love goal-setting or hate it, or find your-self somewhere in between, thinking it doesn't work for you, or you never stick with it, or it all just feels so not creative and fun, I want to tell you to take the time and do this process. It is a very different way of working with goals and intentions, and it is a key component in the creation of what you need, want, and desire.. This has worked for me powerfully over the years. In the beginning, I am giving you a worksheet and a step-by-step process. Someday, this will become not just something you do, but a way of living and being. It will become an automatic part of your creative process.

90 Days Goals and Intentions Worksheet

Many times, in working with coaches, they taught and trained me to work with the 90-Day framework. It's my favorite way to work with my private clients, too, in a 90-Day Private Coaching Program.

In working on specific areas of my life and my business, I learned to create a sacred container of 90 days and work within that. Studies have shown that the momentum and clarity and focused energy needed to work toward a goal or intention begins to dissipate rapidly at anything beyond 90 days. Even as you are creating success, you change so much, and your world changes so much. Everything inside the container shifts, and that is a good thing. But you need to understand how to work with it to create the most success for yourself.

Why ninety days?

This period of time, the equivalent of one season, has been identified as a key period for defining and working on goals and intentions. Starting here today, you are, essentially, working on the business of your life. In 90 days, you can make dramatic and measurable changes in your life. Get clear about your destinations, then discover, over time, the paths you will take to get there. You have the chance to revisit your plan and your purpose and make adjustments; to receive feedback; to act, assess and adjust, making course corrections to move you forward more powerfully to where you want to be. You have the opportunity to reflect on the changes within yourself and your world.

Do not follow your life blindly. Do not live your life by default. Create your life with energy and intention.

Are you merely interested or committed?

Shifting is only the beginning. As you move out of your current experience into creating a new way of being, doing, and having, it requires conscious maintenance of this new state of being you move into so you don't fall back into patterns that no longer serve you. You'll be working at all levels, too, as you integrate the changes you are making physically, mentally, emotionally, and spiritually.

1. To begin using this tool, set today's date on your calendar, and then count ninety days out, and capture that period of time. Intentionally set this time as your sacred container for transformation and success in creating what you need, want, and desire.

2. Set aside some time to get into a reflective or meditative state and ask yourself, what do I want right now? Listen for the answers that come from within from deep inside you. Pay attention to feelings that appear that may not even have clear form to them. Be sure you feel passion about these goals you are going to set for yourself. Do not limit yourself with shoulds or what other people want you to do.

3. Take several deep breaths, and write what comes to you from your heart. Set a timer if that helps. Do not stop writing until you feel complete. Do not reread what you are writing or make any corrections at this time. You can go back later and revise and refine.

A. Number Your Paper 1–10.

List Your Long-Term Goals/Intentions and Set a By When Date.

(In this process, we use deadlines and, at the same time, recognize they are fluid and flexible.)

B. Number Your Paper 1–10.

List Your Short-Term Goals/Intentions and Set a By When Date.

(You may find it helpful to set the Long-Term Goals/Intentions first then break those down into Short-Term Goals/Intentions.)

- After you have filled in all of the spaces, read each one out loud and notice what you feel. Make note of the energy of each goal/intention. Which ones carry a lot of energy? What comes up for you around each one?

- Choose one to three of these that you would like to work on for the next 90 days. Choose more than one if they naturally group together and will be related. Write the goal/intention you have chosen for yourself.

- Now, with the goal(s)/intention(s) you have chosen, break that down into an outer intention and an inner intention. The outer intention will appear to be more of an action and an outcome, while the inner intention will appear to be more of a transformation or a shift that is related to thoughts and feelings and states of being.

- Spend some time reflecting on what you have written here and what you have experienced in doing this exercise.

Make A Decision about this goal/intention, and work with it until it feels just right. Write out a statement:

I Decide _____.

Own It . Offer yourself unconditional support with this decision, whether that is for twenty-four hours, a week, twenty-one days, or ninety days at a time; feel your way into it. Notice what comes up for you, both positively charged and negatively charged. Make note of what you are thinking and feeling and doing.

Visualize It. Your Visioning Tool will greatly support and guide you in working with your 90-Day Plan.

Execute It; Take Aligned Inspired Action. Notice what actions you are inspired to take, what synchronistic breadcrumbs call for you to follow, and what opportunities show up for you to say yes to.

The sooner you take an inspired, aligned action toward what you say you want, the more quickly and easily it will show up in your world.

Great work!

CHAPTER 12

Are You Strengthening Your CORE?

In the beginning, during the first few years I was working on changing my life and building and growing my business, I got results, mostly inconsistent and for short periods of time, and I suffered setbacks. But each success brought celebration and kept me moving forward.

Yet, so many people fall out, and I was tempted to, until I discovered these "4 Steps to Help You Start Strong and Create What You Desire." I had to find a way to manage my energy to maintain the success I was creating.

At the time I created this, I had been introduced to pilates and had restarted my yoga practice, and I started to see how this concept of beginning with a strong core was equally important in how you do life and business.

If your core is weak, nothing else can be strong.

By working first from the CORE, it will make you stronger mentally and emotionally and help you build a rock-solid foundation from which you can create everything else!

As the whole of you works together and is completely interrelated—body, mind, and spirit—everything relies on your core. It's your base, and your center of attraction.

Here's how to start strong and create what you desire.

C. Clarity

Confusion is one of the things I most often see keeping people stuck. Whenever you get stuck in confusion, the first thing you want to do is create clarity. It can feel overwhelming, and you may feel like you're not ready or prepared to get clear. But that's because you are seeing and feeling your big picture, your big Vision. You only need to create clarity around this moment and your next step. When faced with confusion, there is always something you can do to move out of confusion.

Just start with, "What is one thing I need to know?" and when you are able to connect with that information, you can then take an action in that direction.

"I'm confused. I'm stuck." is an excuse. Confusion is a defense mechanism. It does not serve you. It creates a story, and allows you to live in that story, if you choose. It is a distraction, and it is ultimately avoidance.

Recognize it. Own it. Push through resistance into receptivity.

There is always a way forward from wherever you now stand.

O. Ownership

Here we are back to owning it 100 percent! Yes, it's that important.

Getting clarity about the next thing you need to know leads way to an inspired action it is clear you must take next. Now, it's time to make a decision, and then take ownership of that decision. This is so important, because here's where a lot of people start to fall apart. The minute they get clarity and make the decision to take that next step, there is often a moment of euphoria followed by the ego fighting for its life. So, then you start second-guessing yourself, doubting yourself, playing back all the programs full of limited beliefs and toxic patterns, until there you are, spinning again.

It takes a tremendous amount of creative energy to get yourself from here to where you want to be, especially those first few steps. So, you don't need anything draining your energy, and that's what those kinds of behaviors do.

As soon as you catch the clarity and make a decision, support yourself in that decision 100 percent. Sometimes, this takes practice, and, at first, you may only be able to support yourself 100 percent for a few minutes, a few hours, a day. Notice your own self-talk, and notice the stories you are telling others and yourself. It all counts. It all matters.

R. Receptivity

From this new energetic stance, you can begin to receive what you are asking for. Things will begin to show up for you in the physical when you start taking physical third-dimensional action. Get it out of your head and into the world.

Here is another sticking point for many people. You want to recognize that there is a Law of Giving and Receiving. Picture it like the infinity symbol. Some people have their giving blocked, and then there are those who have their receiving blocked. Your thoughts, feelings, behaviors, words, and actions will give you clues to where you stand.

You want to make sure you are open and allowing the good you are asking for. This is a big part of where doing the energetic work first brings you the best results.

E. Embodiment

Do you see what we are creating here? We get clear on what energetic stance to take and what next step we are going to commit to. Without that, none of the rest of this will bring you what you desire.

Once you are clear, you take ownership. You support yourself 100 percent. You hold onto your Vision and revisit it every day. It's your touchstone. All your energy is now being focused to support what you are wanting to create. Picture this as a hose with a strong concentrated spray rather than lots of trickles going off in all directions. Then you open to receive what you are asking for.

It is written in every sacred text, "Ask and it is given." And, it's true. You are always given the opportunity to create what you are asking for. It doesn't always show up in the way you expect it to. It's not always logical. And it's often not comfortable. Nevertheless, don't miss it when it shows up. The clearer you are, the more centered, grounded, and focused you are, the quicker and easier it will all come together for you. Just like anything else, you want to execute it from a strong core.

The next step is to pull that focused energy right into you. Imagine it. Own it. Focus on it. Receive it. And embody it. Become one with it. Become the person who is being what you need to be and doing what you need to do to have what you desire. Call it in.

At this point, it's important to notice where old habits try to overtake you, fears, doubts, worries, anything that tries to pull you off center. And deal with it immediately. Keep coming back to this new energetic stance you have created for yourself.

If you do this, what you desire will already be a part of your energy. It will already exist around you. It's Universal Law that if you desire something, it does exist for you. Wherever there is a desire, a way has already been made. Now you're ready to move into action.

It takes third-dimensional action to create third-dimensional results. It takes massive third-dimensional action to create massive third-dimensional results.

Along with this, I identified three states of being that are integral to the process of creating lasting change. I am always one to turn my own life and everything about my journey into an experiment before I share it with others. So, I've seen this play out in my life many times now. These three states of being for me are Strong Body, Focused Mind, and Open Heart.

Let me give you a few examples of how that plays out for me. At any time, you're going to be stronger in one or two of these areas and weaker in the others. Throughout time, you're going to have some of these where your lessons lie that you know you really have to work on.

For me, the area of greatest struggle and challenge is strong body. It takes a lot of my energy. I really have to work on it. There are times in my life when I've done it. There are times in my life when I needed the strong body, and I intuitively knew to bring something new in, then it would show up.

Some years ago, I was going through a major transition, and I needed to move a lot of energy and create change in my physical body to do what would come next. I was asking for my next step and willing to do whatever that was, and suddenly I had the strong knowing, I'm going to walk a half marathon. What? Shortly after that, a program showed up in my mailbox that would allow me to train for and walk a half marathon. They would take care of so much of it, and I would be giving to charity, as well. I did it. Very soon after that, the space opened up for me to open my healing and wellness center, and things began to fall into my lap.

A few years further back, when I was again going through a major transition in my life and I needed healing, healing more than just what my usual tools could provide, I discovered Nia. Someone brought Nia to my local recreation center just blocks from my house, and the minute I first tried it, I was hooked. I healed so much from that, and it carried me through a major move into a new community where I trained and received my White Belt as a Nia practitioner and teacher. Because I followed my intuitive guidance and the evidence and support that showed up rather than questioning and hesitating, I was so blessed.

A few years ago, I did something really out of the ordinary for me. Again, I needed to move a lot of energy through my body and shake things up within me, and I was led to kickboxing. Surprisingly, during that time, I really liked it. And it opened things up inside of me and then in my life.

When you work on your life from this perspective and in this way, your next steps that come to you do not always make sense. This is where you learn to follow them anyway.

I love to share the story of how I was so busy opening a new business early on. I had just shut the door on the expensive hobby after 18 months, and I was giving it another chance. I had a lot to do. I had partnered with some people and created a holistic spa in my community. I kept getting a nudge to find one of my old high school friends. This made no sense to me, and, at first, I hesitated and put it off. Then, it began to really tap at me, and I wondered if somebody was in danger or needed help. I was feeling that urgent about it. So, late one night, I got on Facebook and looked up my friend. I connected with him, he seemed fine, we said, hey, and caught up on things. While I was on his page, I saw another old friend I knew. He had been a best friend and former roommate of my ex-husband, so even though I had liked him, he was not someone I normally would go out of my way to look up. When he popped up on my friend's Facebook, I reached out and made a connection with him, too. It turns out he didn't live too far from me. I had been away from this area for many years and had just recently moved back close to where we had grown up together.

There I was not long after that working in the new spa, and he walked in the door. He had found me through the Facebook connection and was in the area. I loved connecting with him, and he ended up becoming a client of mine for a while. I was able to help him through some healing of deep loss and pain. As soon as we reconnected and he saw what I was up to, he said he had someone I had to meet. He brought her by my new workspace, and we had an instant connection. She ended up being a client of mine, then enrolled in some of my programs, then became a trusted friend and colleague. We did some masterminding together in a small group, and then partnered on some great business ventures. I was part of a big event that she put together. The blessings I have received from knowing her have been tremendous, and I count her today as instrumental in my journey.

At the point where I decided to walk the half marathon, I had never done anything like that at all in my life. In fact, I had come to a place where I could not walk very far, and I dug in and I worked on strong body, and I walked a half marathon. I trained for my white belt in Nia and got that. After that, I used Nia with my clients and students, during retreats and taught it in the spa. Nia is made up of principles that I have been able to apply to my life that will benefit me for life. If you don't know what Nia is, it is a great form of mind-body-spirit exercise that is much more than that and very powerful.

During the past three years, I have walked with my family— my mother, father, husband, sister and brother-in-law, and brother and sister-in-law, each summer, a journey of 100+ miles, walking the Camino in Spain, then the Via Francigena into Rome, and then The Cotswold Way through England. These walks challenged me physically, mentally, emotionally, and spiritually. I said yes to all of them, because I knew the benefits and healing that they would bring. That is my next book!

You will start identifying the areas where you have the most value and the areas where you have the most limiting beliefs and the areas where you have the most strength and what you consider your weaknesses. You will want to just work on a balance. Over time, you're going to come in and out of that.

If you think about your body as the vessel, the vehicle, the channel, you will recognize the importance of having a strong body. When I work on my body, I have to really use a lot of my energy and focus and a lot of my time, because it doesn't come easy to me.

I'm one who spent many years living from the neck up as if I had no body. When I wasn't living my vision, my mission, my dreams, and my truth, I had a lot of years where I was stuffing that and I wasn't expressing it, and it took a huge toll on my body. Really loving that body and bringing that body back into balance requires decision and commitment. With the work I do now, my body demands so much more self-care. You will find this, too.

I'm so passionate about working on our lives in all areas holistically and addressing everything in our lives that is showing up. No matter what time you think you have or don't have in the world right now, no matter what you want, bring some of it into your life right now. I was not expressing myself fully and authentically, and I was stuffing a lot of things that were calling to me, and, because of this, I had an undiagnosed illness for seven years which further disconnected me from my body. As a result of that, I moved into this whole direction with the work that I'm in now, and it has been so very powerful for me and even more so when I share it with others.

What I'm talking about is not expressing what was inside of me, what was calling to me. It would call to me, I'd get glimpses of it, I might go on a spiritual quest for a short period of time, immerse myself in it, then come back into my life and stuff it down. I created a lot of busyness in my life, and I created a lot of drama in my life, which is what we do when we're not expressing and living what we're meant to and what's inside of us. It wasn't until I actually got into movement, consistent movement, mindful movement, that my life started becoming and has become a life I love that supports me. It wasn't until then that my business actually became a viable business. And it was through taking consistent steps, sometimes itty bitty baby steps, and sometimes big leaps, that I got here and continue to move forward every day.

Always, when I'm working with someone, I tell them, you know yourself best. There are people who are risk takers and people who are not. I tend to be a risk taker. If you're a risk taker, great. You can make some of those big leaps. But, if taking risks inherently stresses you, it will counteract any results you get. Knowing yourself allows you to do what is best for you first and always. I have clients and students who get just as profound of results by taking baby steps, especially when they are consistent. It's all about knowing yourself and working with your own energy.

There are days when I would be having a rough day, and I used to get stuck and frozen and get into crisis, and it could go on and on. Then, I learned how to take a baby step, the smallest baby step, whatever I could muster, just something, and it started the momentum again.

And that is why I really want to get people into aligned inspired action, because it creates a momentum. Every time you stop and start, and stop and start, it's like having to turn around a large ship or a giant jet plane, and you're sending mixed energy and mixed messages to the Universe. I want this, I don't. I'm engaged, I'm not. I'm committed, I'm not.

Once I got into movement and stayed in movement, it got so much easier. Get in motion and stay in motion. Some days that looks big, some months it looks big, other times you feel like, am I even moving at all? Baby steps, energetic, intuitive, physical, all of it together, and the momentum builds. That's when things happen.

Going back to the three states of being, the second one is focused mind. If you think of your strong body as this vessel, and, then, you have a focused mind and an open heart.

Focused mind tends to be the more masculine side of the body. It's getting into action, it is driving things, it's setting goals, and we need this. You can find numerous examples of people who operate out of that masculine side all the time. Then there are people who operate out of that feminine open heart receptive allowing side.

I can tell you what it looks like for me when I'm out of balance, because I've lived it.

First, I need the strong body to be the vessel, and then I need to work with both my masculine doing side and my feminine being, allowing, receiving side.

When I first began building my business, I opened a healing and wellness center in my community. I was building a community, and my passion was to be teaching, to have an impact, to bring people together, to help satisfy what these people needed and help answer these callings. I had such an open heart that I was having trouble using a business mind, and I did not make good business decisions. I ended up running a very expensive hobby. I created financial disaster for me and my family, I had to close the doors on my healing center 18 months later, and it was a huge learning lesson.

What I realized from that is this is what I naturally do. I go in with an open heart. Before building my own business, I was a Therapist. I came from rescuing victims, serving victims, running shelters, giving everything I had to people who didn't have much or had nothing and ministering to people in crisis. I am built for that. I did a lot of crisis and trauma response. It's very rewarding, but when you're giving all of that and you're not making good decisions—business decisions, financial decisions, physical decisions about your own self-care—a lot of service-oriented and heart-centered people get so caught up in serving the other people that they don't serve themselves. You must change your thinking to know that serving the highest good of all includes you. It has to, or it's not the Highest Good.

You might think that would be self-evident, but I am telling you, when I first heard that it was as if I was sitting forever in the dark fumbling, and suddenly someone said, you know, you can turn on the light. What? What!

As it sunk in, so many things began to change for me. And here's the real "secret," when you start serving from a place of serving your own Highest Good, you actually serve everyone else and the world in a much better way. How great is that!

Serving the Highest Good of all includes me! You know those things where you think well, duh, of course, and then you're not living them, and they smack you right upside the head when you hear something like that. This is one of those things.

"Serving the Highest Good of all includes me" was the biggest permission-giver for me. It really rocked my world. It really changed things. It finally made me realize that one of my unhealthy patterns was that I would open my heart, I would give and give and give until I was collapsing. I'd given away all my money, I'd given away all my time and resources, and then my personal life was falling apart, my family was suffering, my body was suffering, my spirit was broken, and I was heartbroken, because I was trying to help people who didn't want to help themselves. And, hey, they weren't giving back to me the way I thought they would. Have you ever heard, you teach people how to treat you?

What I had to do in order to step in and stop the pain and the mess is to come back in with my focused mind and make strong decisions. But to do this, I would have to close my heart. I'm empathic and I always have been, and I can feel other people's feelings. Empathy is a wonderful strength. It can be your Superpower, but it can also be an Achilles' heel. You see, I had a coping skill that did not serve me. In order to open and use my focused mind, my masculine side would ride in to save the day. The first thing it would do was swing closed the door to the heart. The heart is not serving us; close it up.

The focused mind was rarely used when I was in open heart mode. I wasn't allowing it to serve me, so it always came in once I had created a crisis so that I could give myself permission to use it.

Then, when I was out of the crisis mode, my heart would open back up, and I would shut down the mind.

Now, I am living where I am able to more easily balance the mind and the heart. I'm now making those tough business decisions while still having a heart that desires to serve and make an impact, but that heart is also extended to me.

You want to pay attention to strong body, focused mind, and open heart, all of them, and check in regularly to see where you need some extra attention. If your body breaks down, you can't do the work, you can't support the mind, and you can't keep up the energy you need. All three of those work together.

While we're talking about this, I want to share with you this article I wrote:

WHY I MAKE MORE MONEY IN MY BUSINESS WHEN I DO YOGA

by Dr. Michelle Barr

So often, I see my clients and potential clients I talk to bumping up against the same wall, then retreating. They think or hope that when they return to that place, the wall will be gone. It won't. It will be waiting for them. Until they break through it. Then, that wall will never stop them again.

This weekend, I did a Yoga Retreat. I am reminded again and again to pay attention to this vessel that all my work comes through, and to feed myself as I take care of others. This was a lesson lost on me for many years, and I paid a price for it.

The bottom line is, when I am in my yoga practice, I not only feel better, I do better in my business, and I am better for my clients and everyone else in my world.

As I spent the day Saturday on my mat, I had a lot to work through. It wasn't graceful, it wasn't pretty, and my stuff came up. Hmmm, sounds a lot like when I was first in business. Even now, I have days like this.

And it got me thinking, doing this right now can teach me a lot about doing my business.

I GOT ON THE MAT. I laid it down, and I stayed on it. Even when I was uncomfortable. Even when I didn't know if I was doing it "right." Even when I wanted to stop.

I GOT VULNERABLE. I was out there in the open, doing this thing, and other people were watching me. There were people who were better than me, who looked better doing what I was doing. There were people creating better results. I could not let myself get distracted by them, compare myself to them, or judge myself against them. I had to focus on me. I had to work on being better than myself in every moment.

I GOT FOCUSED, CLEAR, GROUNDED, AND CENTERED. I talk a lot about this energetic stance with my clients and students. This is the place to discover within yourself and to return to over and over again. I had to focus on the moment and perform in the moment. I didn't even know what was coming next, if it would be harder or easier. I had to stay clear, shut out the mental chatter, bump up against my resistance, and stay on that mat. Each time I learned something new, I executed it.

I BUMPED UP AGAINST MY EDGE, AND IT CHANGED. Over and over again, I hit my edge, and I pushed through it. I stretched myself, and it let go. So often, I see my clients and potential clients I talk to bumping up against the same wall, then retreating. They think or hope that when they return to that place, the wall will be gone. It won't. It will be waiting for them. Until they break through it. Then, that wall will never stop them again.

I CELEBRATED MY WINS. A few times, I slid right into a pose, and everything clicked. It's a great feeling when something that was giving you so much trouble suddenly happens with grace and ease. I recognize those moments, and I savor them. It's about Mastery, and it takes practice to achieve Mastery. You will always be mastering your craft.

I RESTED AND REFLECTED. At the end of the day, I went into deep relaxation. I reflected on what I had just done and what I had learned, I opened to insights, I paid attention to how I was feeling and what I was thinking.

I got up and left it all on the mat. I was a different person at the end of the day than I was at the beginning of the day. As I shift, everything in my world shifts.

I will return another day, and the mat will be waiting for me, right where I left it.

CHAPTER 13

Are You Activating Your Energy for Success?

ENERGY ACTIVATION TOOL

This is an Energy Activation. The best way to use this tool is to set aside a quiet time and space to receive it. You can read it, then sit quietly in the energy that is created. You can write or journal or speak into a voice recording. You can simply be in the presence of it. You can also record yourself reading it and listen to it over and over again.

When you are ready, take a deep breath, and read this silently to yourself. If you like, you can read it out loud to yourself, also.

Schedule time so that you can go from this process right into using your Visioning Tool for an even more powerful experience.

Energy Activation

Receive this energy activation. Just receive it and allow it to give you whatever you are ready for. Take a deep cleansing breath, signaling your body, we're getting into this place, this open, receiving space. There's nothing I have to do right now. There's nothing I have to think about. I'm receiving this gift. I am ready to move.

Take another deep cleansing breath. All you need to get started is that something you identify that you would like to create. I ask you this, what is one thing that is not showing up in your life that you want right now? Notice what you notice. Before you try to formulate an answer, notice what shows up; a feeling, a picture, a word, an image, a memory? Notice what you notice. What is one thing that is not showing up in your life that you want right now?

For a moment, move away from this thing from a close-up view, rising higher and higher above it, until you find yourself with a bird's eye view. Breathe deeply, see this that you want to create, see this that you want to show up in your life.

Are you in your head? If so, drop into your heart and breathe deeply from your heart's space. Whenever we want something in our life, what we really want is the way we think it will make us feel. What feeling are you reaching for? What feeling are you desiring? Again, notice what you notice. What comes in first?

Somewhere inside, you know. Open to that knowing, be willing to discover it right now, and let it be something that surprises you, that you may not know is there. What feeling are you reaching for? What feeling are you desiring? If you already had this in your life, what would that feel like? What would you feel like? Allow your gaze to get soft, relax into it. Sit with these questions. Rather than thinking of answers, allow whatever is there inside you to emerge. Notice what you notice.

Be in this space, be fully present in this space, and be in this moment in this space now. Remember everything you can about this place, so that you can return here every day. Soak it in.

Be the observer. What do you feel here? What do you see here? What do you sense here? What is going on around you? Who is showing up? Spend some time just being here in this place, looking at what you want to create and feeling what it will feel like to have it.

Now, give that feeling one word. Go with the first thing that comes to you. Give that feeling one word, and ask, what is one thing I can do today to create that feeling for myself? What is one thing I can do today to create that feeling for myself? Let it come in; it's there. Let it come in. It doesn't have to be as big as what it's going to feel like when you have that thing you want to create in your life. It doesn't have to make sense. It's also not necessarily logical. Go with the first thing that comes to you.

What is one thing I can do today to create this feeling for myself?

Now, commit to doing that one thing today, and when you feel that feeling, notice it, amplify it, express gratitude for it. Tell the Universe, "This, yes this, I love this, and give me more. This, yes, this. I love this and give me more." Feel the power of that in your solar plexus, your heart open, fully empowered, guided, clear, and focused, and now commit.

Make a decision. Own it 100 percent. Visualize It. Commit to taking one inspired aligned action, and Execute It.

Breathe.

Be.

Be in it and with it.

I invite you back into your space, focusing your eyes, coming back to this place where you began.

Recognize that you have heard things that you may not even be able to put your finger on. You've experienced things. Things are being awakened inside of you, invoked within you. Allow this now and for the next few days. Notice what comes up, notice what pops into your head. Memories, feelings, energy, dreams, desires, whatever it is, and allow it. Notice it, do not judge it.

Take a few minutes in this reflective space to capture anything about this experience while it is still fresh here with you.

Thank yourself.

CHAPTER 14

Are You Loving What's Next?

I dream my painting, and then I paint my dream.
—Vincent Van Gogh

We need more people painting their dream.
—Me

All over the personal and spiritual development world and the human potential movement, you will hear teachings about and see a focus on Gratitude. It is important, and it is part of a larger teaching about managing your energy, mastering your emotions, and creating a vibration that supports you to allow and receive what you want.

While I am aware of and pay attention to Gratitude, always, it is not a tool that is part of my daily spiritual practice. I will tell you what is.

This or something better! This is the tool that changed my life and my results in so many powerful ways since I first became aware of it, then really understood it, and started shifting into this mindset in every area of my life.

It is about cultivating a mindset and a belief system that knows that if this is not it, that is because something better is. This frees up your mind from so much draining energy and so much self-sabotage, beating yourself up, and essentially getting in your way.

The Gratitude practice is about finding what you are grateful for and amplifying your feelings and thoughts around that no matter what is going on in your life that you don't love or that is causing you struggle and pain. Gratitude List. Gratitude Journal. All are about tapping into things you can find right now to be grateful for. And feeling grateful raises your vibration. And, when your vibration is higher, more of your good can come to you, more effortlessly and easily.

My method reaches higher into the vibrations of Love and Joy, with an absolute knowing that whatever is not working for me right now is for a reason, and what I will receive when I allow it is "something better."

The first time I really saw this in action was when I was young, married, with three children, and something had happened to our home so that we had to move out of it and find a new place to live, very unexpectedly. Right away, I found what I thought was going to be my new home, and I had many reasons why it was a great home for us to move into. We were only moving within our community, so this was about finding the best house for our family and considering which school they would move into.

When we got to the home inspection, we found that there was a significant foundation problem, and my husband was adamant that we not move forward with the house. We were currently dealing with a foundation problem in the same area that had gotten so bad we were having to move.

I was distraught and questioning why this was happening to me and to us. I could not get myself out of this state I was in, and that was not going to get me anywhere in creating what I needed, wanted, and desired. So, I dug into one of the tools that I had not really fully used before. This or Something Better. I took out a piece of paper, and I printed out a picture of the house that I wanted but was not going to have on it. I still left room in my mind that something could shift and change, and we would end up with the house. What I had to do, I knew, was to detach from the outcome and let the Universe bring me the right match. The Universe can orchestrate for you what you could never orchestrate for yourself, much less envision.

I wrote on the paper, "Thank you for this house. Thank you for This or Something Better." I signed my name to it, and I put it in a space where I would see it and be reminded of it. Then, I had to let go and pay attention to breadcrumbs and opportunities. I had to release wallowing in disappointment or fighting with my husband or feeling sorry for myself or allowing myself to fall into a state of hopelessness or despair.

We got more bad news about the house that was not going to be, and I was inspired to get into my car and to drive around the area. I was frustrated, and that was one of the motivators, at first. I started driving in the direction I felt pulled, which was to another side of the community I was not familiar with. We lived in Colorado at this time, and I began driving toward the foothills we could see in the distance. I love sunsets, and I started driving toward a beautiful sunset. I turned into a neighborhood and came around a corner, and I saw children playing in the front yard and a For Sale By Owner sign in the front yard of a house sitting in a cul de sac with a mountain view and a beautiful view of the sunset. Something touched me. I had a knowing to follow up on this. No analyzing or logic was involved here in this moment. I was inspired, and I had a knowing.

I went to our realtor, who had not seen this house in his records, because it was For Sale By Owner. When I showed it to him and told him I wanted to see it ASAP, he was resistant and tried to talk me out of it. He told me that those kinds of sales were problematic, and he didn't want to deal with it. I asked him if he could represent us, and he said yes. I asked him if he was willing to. He said, reluctantly, yes.

Once I saw the house, I desired it, and in a way that was different from the analytical and logical argument I had for the other house that was falling through. One was in my mind, and one was in my heart, my energy, my knowing. On paper, it didn't have some of the things that I had said I wanted or were must-haves.

Another potential problem appeared. We were told we had to move out by a certain date that would be before a closing could be secured on this house. I was inspired. I told the Realtor to ask the people who owned the house when they had to move and if they would rent the house to us for the weeks we needed. Again, he did not want to do it, and he tried to talk me out of it. But, I pushed. I held to my knowing. And the people agreed.

What I want you to see here, as well, is that they had a need and a desire, and I had a need and a desire, and the Universe orchestrated and matched up those needs and desires. This served both of us for our highest and best. They had suddenly found out they needed to move immediately, and we had suddenly found out we had to get out of our current house immediately.

We lived in that house on that street for five years until another serendipitous move, this time back home to Texas, presented itself. During that time, my children had friendships, best friends, a great school, teachers who impacted their lives. I made some close friendships and had my own experiences. We backed up to open space with a view of the mountains, beautiful sunsets we could see from our backyard, and a big park with a lake. My husband met a friend and ended up joining a men's softball team he played on for several years and enjoyed that time so much. All of us were fed while in that house from things that only living in that house could open up for us in that way.

I have many, many stories of this, but the time I am telling you about right now was the first one, and I will never forget it. I can still see that piece of paper in my head, with the picture of the house on it, and the writing that said, "Thank you for this house. Thank you for this or something better."

Many times, I have gotten what I desired using my Treasure Map This or Something Better tool. I manifested the Sebring convertible right off my vision board that was propped up on the nightstand by my bed. Everything in my head at that time told me it was unreasonable, irresponsible, unrealistic, and probably impossible. Until a series of events transpired, and suddenly it was right there presenting itself as an opportunity to me that I said yes to. I would never have orchestrated those events to occur in that way, but that's not my part, that's the part of the Universe.

This is a really important piece, and I started seeing how key it is. True manifesting is a way of living and a way of being more than just something that you do. It is about learning to live within Universal Principles and Universal Law. It is meeting The Field and allowing The Field to bring things to you, rather than you running around in your body, trying to make things happen. Both of these things are possible and both work. One is working hard through sheer will, impressing matter upon matter, a hammer to a nail. The other is impressing energy upon energy and allowing that energy to take form, then responding to the breadcrumbs and the opportunities that show up by taking inspired aligned action.

What I want you to understand is this. Taking action is not how you create what you need, want, and desire, what you're manifesting. Taking action is how you receive it. This is Universal Law. Taking inspired action, taking aligned action, helps you to receive into the physical what is already yours and already there for you.

It just exists in The Field as potential, as possibilities and probabilities. When someone is future telling for you, someone is reading your future, it is important to understand what you are really being told. I see it as three waves. They are reading these waves of probability, of possibility.

And then there are the things that are still outside the realm of probability and possibility for you. You have a choice point in every moment, as does everyone else. Energy is always shifting. That moment of future telling is only relevant in that moment and a short time afterwards, until someone changes something. It is not to tell you what will absolutely happen. It is to show you the energies at play at that time, so that you can work with it to manifest what you need, want, and desire. It is the awareness, understanding, and knowledge you need to engage energetically with it. You are then called to make a decision, own it 100 percent, visualize it, and execute it. That means taking inspired aligned action!

Everything changes, because every single thing and every single person in your life right now is an energetic match to you, or it couldn't be there.

All works together as a way of living and a way of being, interacting with The Field. This is when synchronicities happen, because The Field is sending you back signs and symbols, synchronicities that you are connecting with what you want and what is yours in The Field and pulling it toward you.

That is why your future is probabilities, possibilities, and things outside the realm right now. But each energetic step you take can move that closer to you. You basically have a choice point in every moment, and every choice you make either moves you toward or away from what you want most.

These are big concepts. Continue to open up to them. Absorb it. Let it land. Read about this, and listen to it every day. If your mind is trying to fight you on some of it, you're still getting it. It's normal and natural.

Your mind is a tool. But it is not the master. It is meant to be the servant. Einstein said, "The intuitive mind is a sacred gift and the rational mind is a faithful servant. We have created a society that honors the servant and has forgotten the gift." Your mind is doing its job to keep you safe and alive.

Another key quote for me in response is, "A ship in a harbor is safe, but that is not what ships are built for." (John A. Shedd)

If you are here right now reading this, you are contemplating moving out of that safe harbor toward what's next. Or, you have already moved away from the harbor that was making you feel safe even though it no longer served you, and now you need guidance and direction. I've been there. I've got you.

You can listen to all my teachings and trainings about this on my Loving What's Next Podcast at www.lovingwhatsnextpodcast.com.

Use the #SoulTeach hashtag on your social media to find years' worth of teaching in small bites available to you, or buy my 365-Day Book, #SoulTeach: Your Guide to Manifesting What You Need, Want, and Desire at www.SoulTeachBook.com.

Connect with me at www.facebook.com/michellebbarr, where I show up every day to engage with my community and to talk, teach, and train about these things.

This manifesting what you need, want, and desire requires that you are always doing your part and working within Universal Law, allowing and expecting the Universe to do its part.

Too many people, too many times, say, well, I want to manifest this. I need this. I want this. I desire this. So, when I see all the evidence that it's here, then I'll do my part, and that doesn't ever work. Then, they say, "Why didn't I get what I wanted?"

Understand clearly what is your part and what is the Universe's part. When that gets really clear, and you actually do it, this opens up for you this whole new world that brings with it ease and grace. Again, it can be clunky in the body all the time trying to make things happen and move matter, or you can work in The Field and bring things into form that already exist as possibilities and probabilities, and bring them in closer and make them manifest.

I've done both, and more and more and more, I like to manifest things and have things come in with grace and ease, faster and easier, as a match to what I want.

At first, you're working a lot to manifest what you need. Then, you give yourself permission to manifest what you want. Healers and Helpers can be the worst at this! "Oh, I don't want to ask for too much. I just want to ask for what I need and nothing more." "I don't want to be greedy (a limiting belief that may not even be yours)." "I am only asking for just enough."

Do you know it is also Universal Law that you having less will never ever, ever cause someone else to have more?

When you have more, you can take more and give it to other people, serve others from a full well, and continuously fill your storehouses. What I used to do was to give and give and serve and serve, a lot of times out of obligation energy, until I was run down and out of resources, even at the expense of myself and my family. Then, I would collapse into myself, which could be weeks, months, or more. Eventually, I would get back up, but all that wasted time I was not living my purpose and doing my work in the world. All that time I didn't realize I am meant to live an extraordinary life while I am doing what I am called to do in the world.

Until the time I realized, I have my own pie! You have your own pie. We each have our own pie. There's not one pie, yet so many givers say, "Let's make sure everyone else had a piece." You might not even take a piece at all, because somebody else might need it more that isn't even there yet, or somebody might want a second piece.

Actually, you get to choose whether to eat it all in this lifetime or not. You having less will never cause anyone else to have more. There is no need to feel guilty about that. You have your own pie.

This really played out for me in 2020. At this time, I was pretty fully living these principles while teaching them, coaching people through living them, and traveling all over the world sharing this way of living and being that has changed my life and is allowing me to live a life I love.

It was a tough year for many. For me and my family, we had many blessings. Right before we became aware of a pandemic which set so many things in motion, my husband and I had decided to move back to where we had lived before he had taken his current job. We had just found out we were going to be grandparents for the first time, and I knew then why I had been feeling such a pull back to Dallas. We were house shopping during Spring Break, the week before the world shut down. One of my daughters got engaged that weekend. My daughter-in-law was pregnant with our first grandchild. We were starting to plan my husband's retirement from his lifelong career as a teacher and school administrator. My other daughter had moved out to LA for a big job opportunity right out of graduate school.

As daunting as it all seemed, a week later, when we had made these decisions and set these things in motion, we continued on, living a pleasure-led life and trusting and following our desires. We had been following the breadcrumbs and responding to the opportunities. After all, I knew Divine Intelligence knew this was going to happen in the world at this time.

I don't get hung up on things that appear to be conflicts in my schedule or invitations and obligations that are all presenting themselves at the same time. I say, Divine Intelligence knows my calendar. Then, I live by these principles and practices.

Fast forward to the summer of 2020, when things were really getting heated up. People on Facebook were constantly posting, tell me one good thing that has happened to you this year. And I felt the restriction, the old stuff I have had to deal with for years. Don't be too big. Don't be too much or have too much. Who are you to have more when some have so little? People are hurting in the world; how can you celebrate all you have?

The truth is, 2020 was the busiest year I had ever had. It was tremendously financially rewarding. I made a decision and owned it 100 percent to show up fully, to run to the front lines and help people with what they needed in the ways they could make it work. I had more clients than I usually carried at any time. I was working around the clock. I was fulfilled, even when tired. All my travels had been canceled, and suddenly I had a lot of time available and less expenses to cover.

At first, I felt bad when that question was asked. Tell me one good thing that has happened to you this year. I wanted to shrink. Who was I to have so much when so many were talking about all their losses and their fears, their struggles and challenges, their pains and problems. And there was no end in sight.

People showed up and hired me to help them heal and to help them grow and to help them create. I created small group programs that connected people in meaningful ways when they were feeling so isolated. I served a full load and beyond of private coaching clients.

My coach at the time said, "How good are you willing to let it get now?"

I finally saw I can go out into the world, and I can create all that I need, want, and desire. I live the life I love, do the work I am made to do, have the experiences I am here to have, and lack and scarcity don't make my decisions for me. I have plenty for myself and my family, and I have plenty to help in whatever ways I want to. When I was living in lack and scarcity, and even feeling somewhat noble and self-sacrificing about it, as we are encouraged to do (again, a limiting belief that does not serve you and may not even be yours), I couldn't help either one of us. I had to keep falling out of the game and then build myself back up to get back in there. It was exhausting and came with devastating consequences.

You have to heal your stories. That was big work I did and continue to do. I have more to say about that soon. You have to heal your money stories, your not enough stories.

I did the work. I did my part. Let me plant the seed for you today. I moved myself into a cycle of joy and well-being. My life got bigger and better. I expanded into my what's next. Over and over again.

Were there scary moments? Yes, very scary. I just told you a story about one of them. Back before I really trusted the principles and practices and before I really lived this way all the time, it was all an experiment. And I had not built the trust that I have today - Trust Myself, Trust Spirit, Trust the Process. Trust x 3.

Were some of the things that showed up as breadcrumbs and opportunities that were mine to take action on inconvenient? Absolutely. Were they uncomfortable? Very. Were they sometimes expensive and illogical? All of it. Those are actually the things you must do, when they scare you and excite you at the same time.

The reason they feel illogical, expensive, uncomfortable, and inconvenient is not to put you through some test or struggle. It's because you are not an energetic match for them right now yet. If you were, you would already have them.

What you are feeling is, oh, these skin tight clothes no longer fit. You know, if you've ever been in something too tight, it's like, I can't get my arm out of it. I can't get it over my head. I can't move. I need to M.O.V.E.

Over there, I see this perfectly fitting garment. That's next for me! It feels like it's pushing at my edges. It costs too much money. it's inconvenient; I'll do it another time, a time when I have more . . . I can't do that, my calendar won't allow it. My husband wouldn't want me to do that. My kids need me. I have bumped up against all of those, Y'all!

I have gone through all of these, and I know what you're going through, but I'm telling you, everything you want is here for you. On the other side of it. You could not have told me the life I'm living now. Not only financial freedom, then time freedom, but the most important one for me, the freedom to live the personal and spiritual journey of my dreams where money doesn't make the decisions. I get to be who I came here to be. And, when I do, I am rewarded for it beyond measure in every area of my life.

This is about your life. This is about loving what's next right now, because what you want CAN be yours now.

What can you make a Treasure Map about right now? What's Next? What do you desire that you can expand out into This or Something Better about rather than constricting into, why not this, why not me, why not now?

What can you move with your own energetic efforts from possibility to probability, from outside the realm of being a match to possibility?

Yes, there are times when I have gotten the something better. I always remember these the most. When that happened, it always was, every time. I can count on it!

PART THREE

How to Handle What Comes Up

CHAPTER 15

Are You Willing to Transform?

"How much good are you willing to receive?"

"How good are you willing to let it get?"

That was a question asked of me some years ago, at a time when I was struggling and stuck, and honestly sabotaging myself all over the place.

It's a powerful question, and it hit me. In the middle of all my complaining and excusing and blaming and lamenting, my coach at the time asked me, "How much good are you willing to receive?" It stopped me in my tracks. And it reminded me that I created these problems, and that means I have the power to solve them.

The Law of Polarity says that everything in our world has two sides. Nothing is not whole and complete. There is balance within our Universe. Life on Earth is all about experiencing duality, contrast as it is also called. We learn what we want by also learning what we don't want. There is dissonance, and there is resonance. Once you learn to recognize when they are in play, you can take back your power that you have given away to all other people and things. Everything exists as a duality with an opposite that cannot exist one without the other. If one side of anything exists, the Law of Polarity says, then the opposite expression exists, as well.

This is good news for you!

Together these two seemingly opposing sides are part of the same, and together they make up the whole. One side of anything does not exist in a vacuum. A full circuit must be created. What appears to be opposite and at odds with each other is actually an integral part of the same whole.

All the things you pit against each other, caught in a tug of war, with black and white thinking and room only for the extremes, in reality exist on the same continuum. You can swing from one end of the continuum to the other and often do before coming to rest somewhere in the middle. It is easy to flip between them and be at odds with yourself and others. If you could just see that you can exist at any time somewhere in the middle in a place that better serves you, that is where you will find your power and your solutions. When you choose to fight one side of this or the other, you stay in fight or flight, and it drains you of your energy. You allow yourself to stay in confusion and struggle, you create resistance and shut out receptivity. You are battling with yourself, and it's an illusion.

A continuum always exists, with two seemingly opposing sides and everything in between. The potential is always there for all of it. Yet, you can get stuck at one extreme end and hold yourself there, unable to find your way out. You make choices every day that hold you in the vibrational space you are hanging out in.

It is you who chooses between these opposites. Your mindset determines what is playing out in your world.

How much good are you willing to receive?

I post this often on Facebook, and it always gets a very positive response. It really lands. Seems simple, and most of the time transformation is, except in the messy middle for as long as we choose to stay there.

Do this:

1. Make a list of things that make you happy.
2. Make a list of things you do every day.
3. Compare the lists.
4. Adjust accordingly.

To get to the root of not living a life you love right now and not living your purpose, you have to get to the core of it, and that is what we are going to do.

An Assessment for You: THE 5 CORE ISSUES AND YOUR BIGGEST FEAR–HOW TO STOP THEM IN THEIR TRACKS!

You came into this world as You, with a clear *Soul Purpose*, that when lived, promises to bring you an Abundant Life.

You came into a *collection of people*, environments, and circumstances that created overlays, things that appear to be you but really are not.

You are such an amazing being that *before you could even speak* or understand language, you had the ability to learn from the energies around you, both through what was being said and what was not being said.

By the age of seven, you had *accumulated systems of limiting beliefs* that became your core issues. You bought these limiting beliefs. You bought these programs and allowed them to be installed. As time went on, you aligned with these beliefs which then affected your thoughts, feelings, and actions. And THAT affected EVERYTHING in your world!

You walk around with this *self-created trash* made up of all the things you have chosen to pick up and hold onto along the way. Because of this, you experience pain, sadness, resentment, regret, loneliness, anger, fear, doubt, worry, hopelessness, and despair.

You came to conclusions, and so those conclusions played out in your life over and over again. This strengthened their hold on you, because you see what you believe.

Now, here you are, with these callings, these deep stirrings, gentle nudges, whispers, intuitive urgings, and, sometimes, traumatic awakenings.

You are being called to clear a path to your Soul. When you bring the Self into alignment with the Soul, it creates a congruent energy and allows the Soul to show up, to speak to you and to soar. EVERYTHING CHANGES!

When you feel like you're spinning your wheels; when you keep falling back into patterns that no longer serve you; when you have dreams and desires that are calling to you, and you don't see a way to connect with them and make them a reality—it is the perfect time to clear a path to your Soul, to dig through the trash, clear the mental and emotional clutter, and rediscover the treasure that awaits you.

There are 5 Core Issues that all these limiting beliefs stem from. Imagine a house of cards that builds layer upon layer on itself. Shift one card, and the whole thing comes crashing down.

Use this chart to identify the statements you think and say to yourself the most, then identify the Core Issue at the root of them.

If you strongly identify with more than one, rank them in order. Dig deep. Take honest inventory.

Next, identify your Number One Fear, where you have concluded, I Am Afraid. You were born into this world with only two fears—the fear of falling and the fear of loud noises. All other fears were impressed upon you and incorporated into who you think you are.

Here is where your deepest work begins.
You think and say:

> *I am not smart enough.*
> *I am not strong enough.*
> *I am not good enough.*
> *I am not prepared enough.*
> *I am not ready.*
> *I am not credentialed enough.*
> *I'm not (fill in the blank) enough.*

You concluded: I am not enough.
You think and say:

> *People don't want what I have.*
> *They won't pay for this.*
> *I don't have the right (fill in the blank) to succeed.*
> *My expertise is common sense.*
> *Who would want what I have to offer?*
> *I have nothing to offer.*
> *I can't compete.*
> *People won't hire me in this economy.*

Who am I to do this?
The people I serve have no money.
There are too many people already doing this.
I shouldn't charge for this.
People don't want what I provide.
People won't pay my full fee.
I will have to discount to get clients or customers.
I will have to take less pay to have a job/to have this job.
I'm not as good as (fill in the blank).
I can't take care of myself.
I can't possibly charge that much!

You concluded: I am not valuable.

You think and say:

I'm a failure.
I lack focus.
I can't do this.
I'm not good at (fill in the blank).
I can't handle it.
I'll get overwhelmed.
I don't have what it takes.
I don't have all the answers.
I won't be able to handle it.
I will spread myself too thin.
I can't sell myself.
I'll never make good money at this business/job.
This won't work for me.
I need to learn more.

I have to work too hard to succeed.
It won't be easy for me.
I don't know enough.

You concluded: I am not able.

You think and say:

(Fill in the blank) will leave me.
I will have to leave (fill in the blank).
I am afraid to disappoint (fill in the blank).
I don't want to alienate anyone.
I don't want to hurt anyone.
I don't want to have more than others.
I don't want to stand out.
I don't want to leave anybody behind.
They'll laugh at me.
What will they think of me?
They'll talk about me.
They will disapprove.
People won't like me if I'm successful or powerful.

You concluded: I am not safe without the tribe.

You think and say:

I can't have it all.
I don't really need as much money as I think I need.
I only want enough to get by.
They'll think I'm greedy and inauthentic.
I don't have time.

I don't have money.
I never win.
It won't work out for me, so why bother.
It will cost a lot.
I don't want to be selfish.
I don't want to be greedy.

You concluded: I am not prosperous, and there is not enough for everyone.

You concluded: I am afraid.

I am afraid of not being able to pay the bills.
I am afraid of leaving my secure job.
I am afraid of not doing it right.
I am afraid no one will want what I have.
I am afraid of getting hurt.
I am afraid to be visible.
I am afraid to be vulnerable.
I am afraid of losing it all.
I am afraid of having it all.
I am afraid of failure.
I am afraid of success.
I am afraid to show the real me.
I am afraid of not being accepted.
I am afraid of being rejected.
I am afraid I can't learn how to do it.
I am afraid of not having enough.
I am afraid of criticism.
I am afraid of being overwhelmed.

I am afraid of what others will think of me.
I am afraid of being wrong.
I am afraid of making mistakes.
I am afraid people will think I'm selfish.
I am afraid people will think I'm greedy.
I am afraid people will think I'm (fill in the blank).
I am afraid of asking for money.
I am afraid of making more money than (fill in the blank).
I am afraid of telling the truth.
I am afraid of who I will become.
I am afraid of (fill in the blank).

There are many ways for you to clear, heal, and resolve these core issues and transform your life and your results.

You have only a few core issues, and they are playing out all the time. They are driving your bus if you are not consciously aware of them and working with them. You allow them to build and grow within you into a giant house of cards.

You think you have so many problems to address. Really, it's this one core issue that is at the root of it. The drama, the disaster, the distractions, the despair; it's all tied up in this. Unravel the core issue, and it all comes undone.

This is a big part of my life's work. I have always done deep transformational work with people who show up in my world. I have done this work with people throughout my life as a therapist, crisis and trauma specialist, hospital chaplain, spiritual director, energy medicine specialist, spiritual development coach, and business growth coach.

People would come to me to build a business, find the love of their life, heal a relationship, or create a result they were asking for, and then they would take a deep dive into their stuff, their core issues. AND they would discover that on the other side of this was all the things they really wanted!

Do this work to release what is finite—the limiting beliefs, the traumas, the imprints—and receive what is Truth, an infinite awareness of your Self and Soul and all that is great that you carry inside of you, along with the things you truly desire.

CHAPTER 16

Are You Open to Making Peace with Your Past to Gain Power for Your Future?

A coach of mine at the time asked me if I could believe that, in this moment, I have everything I need. I wasn't sure, at first, but I learned to adopt this new belief and to borrow her belief until I had my own.

You have everything inside of you in this moment that you need. Trust me on this.

It's actually Universal Law. An opportunity cannot show up for you unless you have everything you need to respond to it. The reason it feels uncomfortable and even painful is because it will stretch and grow you to become a match to it. If you were already a match to it, you would already have it. If you desire it, a way has already been made. Your work is to become the person who can get those results.

As I just talked about while going through the core issue transformation, while you were still in the womb, you absorbed the energies of the people you chose to come into the world through. Before that, you chose the lineage of people you would come through.

Once born, you were aware of the people in your immediate environment, especially the people you depended on for survival. Because of your strong drive to survive once here, you quickly learned through the mechanisms already in place how to be what you needed to be and believe what you needed to believe to remain within the tribe.

We are programmed with a strong drive to remain in the tribe. "I am not safe without the tribe" is one of the five key fears I identified for you in that exercise. Leaving the tribe meant death. This has been carried down through our lineage, and we still play it out in many ways. It is hard wired within us.

Before you even had language, you were sensitive to the tones in voices and the energy in the room. You picked up cues about what was "right" and what was "wrong." You picked up ideas and beliefs about money simply by being in the environment and attached to the people.

So many of our stories, when we dig deep enough, include, "our people never," "people in my family always," "the women in our family would never," and so on, and so on.

You picked up what was important and what wasn't, and you created beliefs to support what you were picking up.

These influences are pervasive, and they are hidden, until you do the deep work.

It is so important to be able to identify these things we carry that are not ours and the vows and agreements and loyalties that are playing out within us about them and the people we are attached to.

When you can make peace with your past, shed what is not yours to carry, cut cords with what no longer serves you, and then come back to the family and to the Ancestral Lineage in this cleared space, you can draw on the power in your people and their continued and ongoing support for you and carry that power forward into your future. This means you can draw on their strengths, and you can claim and own the gifts running through your blood. You can connect with those who came before you and allow them to stand powerfully beside you.

In our society, we often focus on the trauma and dysfunction that is passed down through our family. The focus is on how this aspect affects us in our lives now. When I was in graduate school training to be a Therapist, my specialty was generational dysfunction and family systems. No wonder, even in this new realm where I work, I am still drawn to this process. Once I moved into energy medicine and healing, I continued this work through Family Constellations. It is the most amazing marrying of the two worlds I work in.

From the perspective of what I do now with my clients, it is important for me and them to understand that you can heal your Ancestral Lineage of spiritual, financial, relational, mental, emotional, and physical issues you are carrying and draw energy from your Ancestral Lineage to do the work you are made to do and live the life you are meant to live.

Those who choose to do healing in this area of their lives often feel the need to sever or separate themselves from these people and these energies. They do this in order to survive. In doing that, they shut down the gifts their ancestors have for them. In closing themselves off from this, they close themselves off from all of it.

You continue to play out these energies through your family systems, moving from the families you were born from into the families you create for yourself. You actually play out these energies in every area of your life, most often unconsciously, in an attempt to clear, heal, and resolve the underlying issues. By being either unwilling or unable to resolve them at the origin and source, you seek out substitutes, stand ins, to play them out with.

The strengths and gifts of your ancestors and their wisdom are a part of you. They are always with you. You choose to shut them out or access them. When you work on healing yourself, you heal seven generations back and seven generations forward. When you work with your ancestors and their energies, you can transform yourself, your family, and your world.

You have a lot of nonphysical support around you and accessible to you at all times, whether you choose to connect with it or communicate with it or not. All these energies are here for you, but do you understand how deeply your ancestors care about your life and are invested in your time on Earth? Their ability to support you and help you through this life are profound. They can guide you and teach you in very practical and powerful ways. Imagine what strengths and gifts and talents and traits flow through your Ancestral Lineage and through your bloodline. When you allow yourself to open and receive these, you are being more of who you are.

Your Ancestral Line is a part of your power. It runs through you. It gives you the capabilities you need to be here and do the work you are here to do. You are made to do it. The land your ancestors stood on holds power for you. You now are being made aware of this, and you are being called to carry your lineage forward. When you agree, you carry the power of your entire line.

You gain so much power when you learn how to draw energy from your Ancestral Lineage. When you learn how to work with your ancestors through first CLEARING and HEALING and then through RECLAMATION and ASSIMILATION, your world absolutely transforms.

Every generation is called to carry forward the evolutionary trajectory of their ancestral heritage. It becomes their duty to make the best use of their ancestral blessings as they look to the future while healing what no longer serves them from the past. This healing addresses generational dysfunction, trauma, wounds, behaviors, limiting beliefs, resistance, toxic energetic patterns, and ways of being, doing, and having.

As a Soul, you carefully selected a specific family lineage. This lineage was chosen to provide tremendous opportunity for personal growth, spiritual growth, and enlightenment while healing the issues from the past that keep being carried forward until someone agrees to address them and change them. When you are able to break free from the limiting patterns of the past, it will allow your ancestors to break free from their bonds, as well.

Imagine having more ease in your life. Imagine not expending so much energy wrapped up in relational issues within your family that also then carry out into all other areas of your life. Imagine clearing and healing mental and emotional blocks that lead you to the freedom you seek and the journey you desire.

By opening to this, you can learn how to work with this consciously to create what you want rather than continuing to unconsciously create what you don't want by default. You can connect with your ancestors, heal what needs to be healed, reveal what needs to be revealed, and honor them with your own personal practices. Allow the ancestral abilities and knowledge to flow through you when you clear the blocks you have put in place as a way to protect yourself.

A REFLECTION FOR YOU: An Ancestral Clearing and Healing

Come with me on a journey . . .

Imagine a long line of people—all of your ancestors from your mother's side and from your father's side of your family going back for generations, much further back than you remember or have been told about, back until the beginning and beyond. This line winds for miles and miles, running off into the distance, covering ground that changes in its features and its feel.

Each ancestor is holding a straw basket in their hands. Inside this basket is their lifetime of limiting beliefs and fears and ways of thinking that they both inherited and created along the way through the living of their lives. See how the baskets at the back of the line pour into the baskets closer to you, one after the other, all the way up the line.

These ways have accumulated and been passed to each successive generation. Your ancestors feel the heaviness of the weight of their basket. Often, they are tired of carrying it around. They don't know that they can set it down, and they wouldn't know how. They know that what is inside is not good for them or those they pass the contents on to. Yet, it is theirs. It is a part of the legacy. It is the agreement made by the members to remain in the tribe. It is a matter of pride. We survived in spite of this. We made it through carrying this. We are that kind of people. This is what our people do.

Hands over heart, feeling your own power strong in your solar plexus, pull up from the Earth all the grounded and centered support you can, then pull from Source, way, way up, all the unconditional love you can. Send that energy from your heart down the rows touching the heart of each one of your ancestors. Spirit is assisting you in this, so it flows continuously and happens very quickly.

In this energy, you are releasing yourself from continuing to carry what is in these baskets, and you are thanking them for carrying them for so long. You invite others to step into this energy with you and put down their baskets, and they may, or they may not. Watch it happen. Do not cause it to happen.

A fire burns brightly before you, in between the two lines of ancestors, and everyone is invited to toss these baskets and all their contents into the purifying fire. The fire burns bright red, and as it fills, the flames begin to transform into a violet flame. Allow the violet flame to wash over you, transforming all the energies to neutral and returning them into the void, back to Source to be transmuted.

Once you feel complete with this, look again down the lines, gaze into the faces, feel the energy being reflected back to you. You chose to come into the world through these lines. You chose the parents who brought you into the world. All of this has gifts in it.

You say to them, "I love you. I'm sorry. Please forgive me. Thank you."

Now, you hold before you an empty bowl, a blessing bowl. You lift it up and hold it out toward them. You feel your energy opening to them, and you invite them to fill your blessing bowl.

As the monks came down into the village each day and held their empty blessing bowl for their community to fill with gifts and blessings, so you do that now with these people, your people.

What they offer you now is their strengths and their gifts, their wisdom, and their knowledge gained from their lifetime experiences. They bring you the positive traits passed down through your family lines. They bring you the most of your people when they are at their highest and best. Feel as they fill your bowl with their blessings and gifts. These offerings come from the power of love.

In return, once again connect with the strength and support of the Earth, letting the roots come out from the bottom of your feet and travel deep into the ground. Reach your energy up out of the top of your head, connect with Source, and pull the unconditional love and Source energy back down. Send this Energy now flowing through you out of your heart and down the lines of your ancestors.

See an infinity symbol forming in the space between the two lines, and the energy begins to circulate from you to them, from them to you, to them, to you.

Pull your energy from below you back up into your body. Pull the energy from above you back into your body. Pull your heart energy back into your body.

Allow the ancestors to move away from you now, as you imagine a bubble of pink light coming down over you and surrounding you until you are inside of it. Inside this bubble, you and your energy are contained. You give everyone back their energy with love and light, and you take your energy back. Feel what that is like, to be in your own energy. You are not carrying the weight of others. You are not bound by outdated agreements. You are here to fulfill your purpose, and you are supported.

If you would like me to lead you through this process, you can find a video of me live streaming this at a retreat that you can use over and over again. You can find it by searching "youtube Ancestral Clearing and Healing with Michelle Barr" or, "Facebook Ancestral Clearing and Healing with Michelle Barr."

At one point in the journey, I instructed you to say to them, "I love you. I'm sorry. Please forgive me. Thank you." You may or may not recognize this as the Ho'oponopono Prayer. This is a very powerful clearing and healing tool that I have used for the past 16 years to dramatically change my life.

Ho'oponopono is based on the key principle of personal responsibility, and, with great responsibility comes great power.

Before I could ever begin to build this life that I have now, I had to work on me, specifically on all the mental and emotional clutter that was preventing me from receiving inspiration and stopping me from acting on it.

The truth about limitation is that it's all self-imposed. As The Fairy Godmother points out to Cinderella in one of my favorite songs, "Impossible things are happening every day!"

We receive information in two ways. We receive information from data, and we receive information from Divinity. How clear we are of the mental and emotional clutter and how well we have trained ourselves to stop reacting, and respond and create instead, determines which way we most often receive the information we need to live our lives and create what we want and need.

When we receive our information from data, we are reacting from our past programming and conditioning. When we receive our information from Divinity, we are receiving inspiration straight from Source. This is the kind of information that moves us forward, where the data is what keeps us stuck and stops us in our tracks.

This tool and practice has been invaluable to me in creating a life I love and everything I need, want, and desire to support and sustain it. I now only do what I am made to do, and as I grow and evolve, my life grows and evolves, as well.

Ho'oponopono is a prayer, four simple phrases:

- I Love You
- I'm Sorry
- Please Forgive Me
- Thank You

The key is the intention behind it that shapes the energy and directs it. Too many people are always focused on everything and everyone outside of them. If this person would change, if that person would do different and be different, if these people would just stop this or start that, then the person projecting all this would be okay. You are trying to make others change because they make you uncomfortable. No one else is responsible for your happiness. You cannot make anyone else change. When you are locked in a dance with someone else, you can choose to stop doing the dance, and this will cause them to have to change. You just don't get to choose how they change. Everyone has freewill.

Using Ho'oponopono, you are always clearing yourself. You are clearing away the data, the programming and conditioning you are acting from. You are making a way back to the Zero Point, the Zero Field, the creative void where all possibilities exist for you. Imagine you have a white board; you write on it all the things that are your stuff, your crap, and then you wipe the board clean.

You are always working on yourself. If someone or something is showing up in your life and your world, something in you is needing them to, so you clean on what is inside of you that is creating them. When people come into your world, you hand them scripts and ask them to put on costumes and play out your stuff with you. When you take responsibility for cleaning and clearing your own stuff, they are released from this and can show up to you in other ways. They no longer are stuck playing this out with you, and you are able to experience other facets of them, especially the ones that you do want.

Choose something that keeps showing up for you. Ask yourself, what am I creating that I don't want? Identify what this thing is, how it is making you feel, and who you are playing it out with. Next, ask yourself, "What inside of me needs them to show up like this right now?"

You don't have to know the answer.

Say the prayer until you feel a shift in the energy, even if it is temporary.

Every time you feel this come up, do it again.

Every person is a diamond with many facets. Most often, we are first attracted to them by the facets that light up that are a match to us in ways we like and love. This is why we experience the "honeymoon period," with both lovers and friends, as well as with new jobs. After some time, as we are engaging in energetic exchange with others, we begin to light up the facets within them that are a match to our own mental and emotional clutter, our own conditioning and programming, and we play it out with them until we go back to its origin, to the core issue, and clear, heal, and resolve it there.

This is a complex concept I am laying out for you here. It is my intention that you open up to it and are nudged to explore it further. Then, you can seek out people to help you and find the clearing and healing tools that work best for you. I have studied and trained in many, many healing modalities over the years, I have not been without a coach since 2009, and I have taken the best of what works for me and integrated it into my daily spiritual practices, my daily business practices, and my life. This is the transformational work I do with my clients, and if you are led to do this work with me after reading my book, connect with me at my website, and we will schedule a time to talk. You can send me a message at www.michellebarr.com/contact-dr-michelle.

> *When we begin to dream big dreams, to set intentions and goals for ourselves, when we begin to strive for prosperity, abundance, health, wealth and success, everything that is not in alignment with that rises up to be healed or transformed. We must heal so that we can soar.*

To really apply this and live it, you have to go deeper, you have to take this theory and live it in your life, you have to develop practices, use the tools, and do the inner work. These are some of the tools that have stayed with me. They are my go-to clearing and healing tools, principles, and practices. I have a mantra that my friends and family love me to share with them, and they love to watch it in action in my life. They especially love to travel with me to see it all happening in real time and to benefit from it, as well. I have them now using it for themselves. I tell the Universe, "Universe, Surprise and Delight Me!" And it does. Over and over again. Along the way, as I did the work and followed the breadcrumbs, acted from inspiration, cleared, healed, and resolved my crap, the Universe has surprised and delighted me with ever more.

As I began to clear, heal, and resolve all that was in my way, running the show, and driving my bus, I began to hear the whispers and feel the nudges. I was able to start seeing the opportunities. They still felt uncomfortable, inconvenient, and often seemed illogical, but I came to trust them. I followed the breadcrumbs. And a whole new world opened up to me! "Tell me, Princess, now when did you last let your heart decide?"

These Ancient Wisdom teachings still apply today, and they are available to you through me and others who are ready to cross paths with you. When you are ready. You are holding this book in your hand. It showed up in your awareness. You are reading it! That's a great sign. Keep Swimming.

CHAPTER 17

Are You Going to Drop Your Money Story and Fund the Life of Your Dreams?

W e're talking about trusting your desires, about following your desires, about leading a desire-led life. Do you know that most people spend the majority of their time using pain as a motivator even though they wouldn't do that consciously?

They use pain as a motivator. They stay where they are. Our brain will seek out, this is like this. It will keep us in places and recreate circumstances that we already know how to survive, even when it no longer serves us and isn't good for us. This recognition opened up so much for me when I truly understood it.

Our brain and body are wired and designed to keep us safe and alive. Manifesting what you need, want, and desire is about rising above the mind and not letting the body and the mind control everything. It requires getting into and staying in a higher state of being.

People will stay in the pain because it's comfortable and familiar. They already know they can survive it. When the pain gets bad enough, they use pain as a motivator to move. I did that for years and years. Pain, drama, distraction, chaos; those were the things that moved me or didn't.

When I knew better, I did better. For years now, I have been committed to living a desire-driven life, which means I trust my desires and know they were put here by my Soul. When I trust my desires, I trust the Universal Principle that, "Where there is a Desire, a way has already been made."

I learned to not wait until I was in pain to move. I stopped moving away from my pain when it got bad enough, and, instead, I started moving toward my pleasure. Guess what happened when I did that? I no longer allow myself to get in pain. I stopped creating so much pain, because I no longer needed it as a motivator. I stopped going there.

I never ask you all to do anything that I haven't done first. I always go first, I walk through the fire, and then I turn around and share with you from the other side of it. This is literally how I have created this business I have had for 16 years now. I tell you with 100 percent certainty, "Where there is a Desire, a way has already been made." When you can start telling yourself that, you can start inching out and stepping out, first in baby steps, then leaping off some ledges, and then creating those big quantum leaps toward your desires.

I don't have to be in pain physically, mentally, emotionally, or spiritually, because I stay ahead of that game by following my desire and my pleasure.

Here's a principle I want to share with you, because you may be asking questions that this will answer, or it may be getting in your way. You always have to go first, and here's why. We came to Earth with an agreement with Divine Intelligence and the collective and all that is that we have freewill while we are here. Otherwise, you'd come down here, and you would be a puppet. Remember, it's always both sides of the coin. Both have to exist simultaneously. If you want to be able to create all that you need, want, and desire, you have to be responsible for all that is created by you here.

You have freewill. Divine Intelligence cannot and will not impede on your freewill. All manner of unseen guidance can whisper in your ear, tap you on the shoulder, nudge you, send you signs and symbols, and cheer you on. But Divine Intelligence cannot rush in to meet you until you make a decision and take action, third-dimensional real-world action. That means, not just, I decided . . . A decision has not been made until an action has been taken.

In order to manifest, it is important to understand this Universal Principle, "Whatever you say is, IS." You have to heal your stories. You have to heal your money stories, your not enough stories, all your stories about lack and scarcity and can't and shouldn't, and not and never, and not now.

You grew up with and you were programmed and conditioned with one of these three beliefs: not enough, just enough, or more than enough. When you can look back and identify which one plays out most for you and where it came from, it will be really helpful in you moving forward toward what you desire.

Not enough is, there's never enough, or it comes in at the last second, you have to beg for it, and there's sacrifice, you need to learn to settle, or you need to learn just not to have it.

Just enough is, there's always just enough, and, again, it comes in at the last minute, and you're not sure when it will come in or how or if, but it comes in, and your prayers are answered, and you finally have relief.

More than enough is, having what you need and more beyond that. Your storehouses are full. You have more money than month rather than more month than money. You have money in the bank, and the bills are paid, and you can still go out, take that vacation, or buy something for yourself that you want but don't need.

After that, it's increasing levels of more than enough. I had a mentor of mine teach me when I was struggling with money and my stories that financial freedom is not how much money you have in the bank. Financial Freedom is knowing how to make the money you need and want when you need and want it. I took that to heart and worked on myself to achieve this state of being.

Living in a state of being of more than enough is possible. You are what's in the way. A lot of people bump up against this, when they reach more than enough money. Often, they will quickly get rid of it or lose it, because their consciousness and their energy cannot hold it. You hear the stories of so many people who won the lottery and lost it just as fast.

Do I dare have more than enough?

Do I dare sit there with a full bank account with my storehouses full while other people have nothing or very little?

These are the thoughts I bumped up against deep into 2020.

You start settling and staying in that programming and conditioning that keeps you in not enough or just enough. Many people are so used to surviving never enough that they really bump up against themselves when they are able to get to just enough.

People get more than enough and then get rid of it very quickly. Or they will have a series of things happen to eat that money up.

Oh good, now I'm back to just enough, because I would not want people to think that I'm greedy, selfish, that I have more than enough. It is self-sabotage for self-protection.

Imagine you're ordering a pizza. It's going out into the Universe. You've asked for this on your pizza and you expect it's going to show up at your door or at the table or out of the oven, and that's your pizza and that's what's going to be on it. It's very straightforward.

But we have all these subconscious programs playing out, and we have all these other orders that sneak into our pizza. So, when you're looking at what is showing up in your life and in your world, you want to notice and look at everything that is showing up. See what is showing up that you do want and what is showing up that you don't want.

Divine Intelligence is saying, yes, you can have everything you want and need. Here's what needs to be cleared, healed, and resolved for you to have it. What is showing up that matches what you need, want, and desire is what you are already allowing and open to receiving. What is showing up that you don't want is showing you what needs to be cleared, healed, and resolved so that you can allow and receive what you are asking for.

When this shows up, these things we don't want, people often misinterpret the message here. It is powerful feedback, but they misread it and construct stories about it that become very powerful in a different way. It's not the right time. God said no. This always happens to me. They don't stay in it and hold the energy and get past it. They don't work with what is showing up. They collapse in on themselves and fall back into their stories, find evidence that it can't be theirs, and create new even more powerful stories that do not serve them.

This what you don't want often shows up first, and it stops people in their tracks.

What will happen here is that you'll bump up against that wall. If you turn around and walk away, no matter when you come back, that wall is still there waiting for you to clear, heal, and resolve what is in the way. Once you bust through that wall and you get to the other side of it, you'll turn around and find that the wall is no longer there. It was energy and an illusion. That wall will never be there again.

Right here, right now, do you dare to connect to one of your desires and see it through the process fully?

If so, there is no second guessing, no self-doubting. You make a decision and own it 100 percent. No saying, yeah, but that could never happen to me, that won't happen to me, I don't deserve that, I'm not good enough, or, I can't have that.

Remember, whatever you say is, IS.

You might have been programmed with, nobody in our family ever . . . the people in our family always . . . people in my life don't . . .

These are stories, and they don't serve you. They may have happened to you, but the worst thing you can do is create a powerful story around them and expect them. You are a powerful creator!

These stories are things that you don't have to live by. You can break those generational patterns and beliefs and behaviors that you have picked up and agreed to carry forward. You can, instead, have what you want. You can bust up these energies for yourself, for the life you want to live, for others in your family, and future generations.

You are choosing along a continuum in each choice point moment to move either toward or away from what you say you want, to create consciously or unconsciously.

When you keep these things hidden, you keep them in the basement, they're still driving your bus. You're not looking at them, and you're not listening to them, and you don't want to know about them, those shadows and those toxic beliefs and patterns and conditioning and programming.

All these things your brain has made up into stories in order to make sense of them, and they don't feel good. So, you store them as energy in motion—emotion—and they take up residence in your tissues and cells. They create dis-ease, and the stress of that eventually creates disease. Your brain becomes a computer, recalling it all, just regurgitating what it knows, unless you rewire it and feed it something new, unless you take control of it. Your brain will just keep reminding you that you better not do that, last time you did that you failed, and remember Uncle Jack, the whole family talks about him, he tried that, and it didn't work for him, it doesn't work. Don't do it. It's too dangerous. So, you believe it, and you stuff it all down, and it keeps driving your bus, and you keep having the same thoughts and feelings, and you keep taking the same actions or not, and you keep getting the same results. The stories grow more powerful, and you spin in it, seeing no way out. Your mind tries to tell you, this is just the way it is for you. Shh . . .

You have a Money Story! There is no question. My question, is your Money Story serving you or not?

Your Money Story is attached to your energy, and you are attached to it. It can be the best scapegoat for you, allowing you to make excuses, and come up with objections for why you can't, shouldn't, won't take aligned action toward what you say you want most.

It's a story created by you, and you are living within it.

You can see why it's essential, then, that you identify your Money Story, take honest inventory to answer the question, is it serving you or not, and then take responsibility for creating and living a Money Story that works for you rather than against you. It's time to get really honest with yourself if you are dragging around that dirty old security blanket because it is comfortable and familiar, even though it is no longer serving you.

For years, I had a Money Story, and I couldn't stop living it. I prayed, I said the affirmations, I wrote in the journals, I took the courses, I read the books and watched the videos, and still I was there in my money story, living it and not loving it.

Once I began taking an honest look at my Money Story, I saw that for over twelve years, from the time I changed my career to be a Therapist, thus living out my purpose as a Healer in the first way I knew how, until I left my last job, I had created circumstances that aligned with my story and then lived it out. In every job I had, I never received money directly from the people I was helping. I was always paid by government grants, donations, and insurance. I had never seen it before, until I saw it. A big part of my story was that it wasn't right to "take" money from people when they were hurting. It also told me that it was okay to receive money for my work as long as someone who "had the money" was paying for it. This caused me to view the people I was helping as "victims" and to disempower them.

Some years later, when I was first building my coaching business online, I was in the "hot seat" in a mastermind with my coach and my colleagues, and she called me out when I said, "When I am taking money from my clients . . ."

"Hold it right there!" she said. "You feel that you are taking money from your clients? That statement was heavily charged." She was right. The way I had said it, you could feel the energy coming off of me, and you could see my body language. I viewed that I was somehow "taking away" from my clients when they paid me, and it was affecting me. I still had that Money Story playing out, even though I had now set up a business where the people I helped were the ones paying me directly. I was still somehow seeing them as "victims" and myself, then, as the perpetrator, taking their money. And I couldn't let myself do it, despite my huge strong desire to serve others in their own healing, transformation, and success.

This is the shift I had to make. I do not take money away from people when they are hurting. People choose to invest in themselves through me for themselves. I am the vehicle for that, and this investment is a key part of the transformation.

I thought about how I had been investing in others for my own healing, growth, personal and professional development, and how me making those investments was a part of the process that created the results. If it is Truth, then it is true all the time for everyone.

Once I was able to become aware of how I was playing this out in my business and drop this Money Story, the way I worked with my clients changed dramatically. Clients started showing up, happy to pay me, often paying in full, and they were doing the work and getting the results. They were transforming, because I had transformed first.

At the time, I was offering complimentary consultations to speak with potential clients and explore how I could best help them. I realized after much frustration that I had another problem with Money Stories. The next level of growth for me emerged.

I was falling into my clients' money stories, and that was not serving them at all, or me.

Potential clients would get on the phone with me. Many would say they knew I was their coach, they wanted to work with me, they needed to change now . . . but, money. There were tears and stories, and I fell into those stories. I supported them in those stories, until I realized what I was doing, and I learned not to. Falling into their money stories was me not showing up as the coach and healer I am. No wonder they weren't hiring me. They were more certain of their money stories than I was that I could help them. They were convincing me, and suddenly they were victims, and I wanted to save and rescue them or let them off the hook. It's an old story for me, one I have thankfully just about done away with. It tries to creep in every now and then, but I am so much better now at catching myself.

Those people getting on the phone with me needed me to meet them at their "no money" objection and see what was really underneath it. I was told by so many coaches that when people say they don't have the money, it's not really the truth and it's not the full story. It's an excuse. It's that dirty security blanket they are dragging around that they wave in front of them when things get uncomfortable. Talking about money makes people feel uncomfortable. It kicks up their stuff. They are coming to me to help them through it, not to fall into the hole with them.

I didn't always believe what those coaches said, until I had it happen to me once, and once again, and once more. People who told great big stories about having no money and "if only" would then go and hire and pay someone else. People will find the money for what they want and need and what they see value in. I was not seeing my own value and worth, I was not standing in it, and I was not believing it, so how could they? Those were some hard lessons to learn, some bricks to the head, as I like to call them.

When I discovered that financial freedom was really all about knowing how to create the money I needed and wanted when I needed and wanted it, everything changed. Freedom is my highest core value. It always has been. But when my Money Story was running the show, it got buried. It didn't stand a chance.

Financial freedom is not about how much money you have in the bank. True financial freedom is knowing how to make the money you need and want when you need and want it.

I made a decision when I became clear and committed that money was not going to make the decisions in my business, and it wasn't going to make the decisions in my life, especially where my personal and spiritual journey was concerned. I learned how to create a vision of the life I wanted to live and then create everything that supports and sustains it. I learned how to make decisions and commitments based on what I needed and wanted and then create the money for it.

Here is a hack I found that works wonders. When I talk to potential clients now, and they say, yes, but, no money . . . I teach them this. I urge and encourage you to try it, too.

New Money Tool

When I find something that I want or need, I never say, "I can't afford it," or "I don't have the money." I believe that, "Wherever there is a Desire, a way has already been made." It's Universal Law. We can count on it.

I find out how much money it is going to cost me, so I know exactly what I am manifesting. When I have to ask someone what it will cost me, I say, "Tell me how much money this is so I can create it." It is all about energy and intention.

Then I go to the Universe with my CLEAR ASK. I say, "I am creating $X.XX for this. I do not want to use the money I already have, because it is earmarked for other things. I am creating new money for this." Next, I become hyper alert. I watch for opportunities to show up. I know they may feel uncomfortable or inconvenient, and they may seem illogical, but I follow the breadcrumbs, regardless. Sometimes, money will show up pure and simple. Other times, the opportunity to create or receive money will show up. At times, both happen simultaneously.

I trust the money is there for me, and I stay in that energy. When I have taught this to a potential client while on the phone with her, often it works pretty quickly, and I get a call or a message that the money did come in, and now she is ready to start.

Take my advice here! When you do this, and the money comes in, you need to keep your agreement with the Universe, and put that money toward what you asked for. This can be tricky if the money comes in, and then you find an immediate need, or your money story kicks in, your fears start whispering to you, and your programming and conditioning plays loudly in the background. You might very well be tempted to take that money and do something "reasonable" or "responsible" with it. Do you want to shut off the flow? You made a CLEAR ASK, and the Universe delivered. When I receive the money, from the first dollar to the last, I put it all right away toward what I asked for. I keep my agreements with the Universe. And I do my part.

Money is energy, and it is neutral until we give it meaning. You and money are in an energetic relationship. It touches everything that is important to you. How you treat it will reflect back on how it shows up for you, or doesn't.

You can start to identify your Money Story and the ways it's not serving you by tuning in to how you are feeling and what you are saying when money comes up. Notice your first response. Hear the stories you start telling. Pay attention to how others talk about money that are around you. Take note when you allow money to make your decisions and override your desires, your gut feelings, your nudges, and the callings of your Soul.

Creating a new awareness is the first step. Facing these money issues and your money crap head on is a great start. Then, it's time to work on your money mindset. Identify whenever you are slipping into Poverty Consciousness.

Once you have done this, you are ready to create a new Money Story for yourself, one that serves you. You begin by creating it, and scripting it. Then, you start telling it. You take aligned action toward what you say you want most. You step into the river of The Law of Giving and Receiving if you are not already in there. You stop playing the When/Then game with the Universe. You do your part, and you trust that the Universe will rush in to meet you, when you go first. You always have to go first.

While we're talking about this, I want to share with you this article I wrote:

THE UNIVERSE DON'T PLAY THAT GAME
by Dr. Michelle Barr

I know this stuff. I teach this stuff. I coach my clients through this stuff. And, alas, I have to live this stuff!

The year 2013 was a tough year for me. I thought it was going to be my breakout year, and, instead, it turned out to be my breakthrough year.

I was teetering glcefully on the edge of a much bigger business and a bigger expanded life. Things were going great in 2012. I had leaped off some ledges, and I was flying high.

You will hear me say that I attribute a large part of my success to making the decision to hire my first business coach in 2009, and I have not been without one since. At the end of each year, I am in search for my coach for the new year.

I didn't know what I didn't know, so I came into 2013 with some skewed thinking and some off-track perceptions about what I most needed right then. I was seeing success up close and personal. I had a big goal I wanted to achieve in this new year, and I went for it. I made some big mistakes, and I learned a lot.

What clouded my judgment and kept me from that next level of success was a story I was holding onto and allowing to have power over me, my life, and my business. My husband and I had made a big lifestyle move, preparing to be empty nesters, and creating the life we wanted to live in this next stage of our journey together. Everything was going great. But something happened with the house we were living in before, and things stopped going the way we had planned.

We had a house, a much bigger house, because the sale had fallen through at the very last moment, when the money should have been pouring by direct deposit into our bank account, and we had to keep paying for it and maintaining it, stuck in the past, while trying to move forward into this wonderful present we had created for ourselves. Everything in our current world was completely aligned and delivering us the life of our dreams, while we kept being pulled back into the past with this house. I got stressed, and angry, and I created a story about it which followed me into 2013.

"I can't hire the coach I really need right now, because that house won't sell." "I can't join the program I really need, because the house won't sell." "I can't get that great office I have always wanted, because the house won't sell."

It held me back. I told the Universe the story, and, so, it was.

I struggled all year long. I hired coaches that were not the coach that I needed and wanted. I put off making the best decisions for my business. I played it small. I played it safe. I played it wrong. And it started affecting my life. As the story grew bigger, it created more and more sorrow and pain for me.

Until I had finally had enough. And I had to drink my own medicine.

I had a lot of private clients in my coaching program and students coming into my group programs. What was I telling them? What was I speaking to others at retreats and meetings, on telesummits and radio shows, on my podcast and on my weekly TV segment?

I allowed myself to stay stuck for way too long, and then I had enough. I pulled myself out of my story, and I looked at what I teach and what I believe. I did the hardest thing. I made a decision. I owned it 100 percent. I believed, and I took action. And that's when everything in my world and my business changed! Only then did the Universe conspire on my behalf.

I had to laugh. Of course. I knew it all along. And I could have done this earlier, but I chose to learn the lesson. I will say, it served me so well as I marched full speed ahead through the year. What I learned was invaluable. It had to be.

Within days, I got a free ticket to an event from the coach I really wanted to hire. I knew this was the push I would need, so I made the trip happen.

I came home, and I took the next step. I hired the coach. It was scary given my current circumstances. And here's what happened next . . .

Within twenty-four hours, I got a new client that paid me double what my deposit for the coach was. And, after that, four more new clients showed up, enrolled in my private coaching programs and paid me in full. The amount of money that came in that week covered the costs of this coach for the entire year.

When I stepped up, the clients stepped up.

Then, an office space became available where I had been wanting an office for several years, and I took it . . .

> *. . . and then my house sold!*
> *. . . and I got more new clients showing up, ready to get started and paying in full!*
> *. . . and some extra money came in that we had been waiting on for 10 years!*

What story are you telling the Universe right now about how it is that is not serving you?

I tell my clients and students all the time, you can't play the when/then game with the Universe. So many people have come to me over the years telling me when I have all this taken care of, when I have all this come in, when I have all this in line, then I will step out and live my Purpose, answer my calling, build my business, quit my job, pursue my passions, and do what I am made to do.

The problem is, that will never work. I have never seen it work yet. And, believe me, I used to try it, too. All it created for me was a lot of pain and struggle and confusion. You are always asked to take the first step. Then the Universe will rush in to conspire on your behalf. All manner of things will show up in response to assist you.

CHAPTER 18

Are You Ready to Connect with Your What's Next?

If I were to ask what you truly want, what would you say? If you don't know, then I hope I have inspired and motivated you to find out. I urge and encourage you to rediscover your true desires, to start moving toward your pleasure rather than waiting to be moved by pain, and to create a life you love that gives you everything you need, want, and desire.

Begin This Trust Journey x 3

Learn to Trust Yourself, Trust Divine Intelligence, Trust the Process.

Every single thing in your experience, every thought, every feeling, every action or non-action, every decision, every move is either life enhancing or life depleting. It either moves you toward or away from what you want.

Whether you are looking for some midlife magic, are wanting to manifest more at this age and stage, in this season; whether you are seeking an early retirement or more money for a future retirement; maybe you want an encore career that better serves you in every way, or you have a heart-based project that has been on the shelf or the back burner for too long; it could be you are looking to reinvent yourself after a divorce or renegotiate your life as a new empty nester, your What's Next is available to you, and it starts now!

I have stood in all these places and moved forward from them. I am still in the middle of my own process in some of them. I wrote this book for you, because I have been where you are, I have walked through the fires, and I am equipped both personally and professionally to support and guide you on our own journey to your What's Next.

The best way to predict the future is to create it. I hope I have shown you how to move yourself out of your own way and be the Powerful Creator you are, so that you can create the next chapter of your life with a new sense of purpose, confidence, and deep fulfillment. There is nothing else like it. It blesses and rewards every area of your life.

Once you realize that The Highest Good of All has to include you, or it's not the Highest Good, you can change your trajectory to the highest and best path for you that is a blessing to others the more you live it.

As I help you to topple the House of Cards that has held you prisoner to your core issues and help you to bust down the wall and get to the other side of it where you can truly thrive, I hope you will know the mountains you have been carrying, you were only supposed to climb.

> *These mountains that you are carrying,*
> *you were only supposed to climb.*
> —Najwa Zebian

It is time to believe in your own creative power and take that power back.

It is time to uncrimp the hose that is holding your abundance from you.

It is time for you to have your heart at ease with who you are.

It is time to M.O.V.E. on to What's Next.

- Make a Decision
- Own It 100 percent
- Visualize It
- Execute It

I am called to start a movement, a Personal Wellbeing Movement, a stop living in Poverty Consciousness movement, a "Why are you still living your life by default?" movement.

I was afraid when I first realized the message I am called here to bring is so big and so bold. Sometimes it upsets people, it makes them angry. I lost one of my really good friends because of this. She said what I was talking about on my social media was just too much. It made her feel bad. I didn't apologize. I let her go. I had to. But, it hurt.

Of course, there was a time when I couldn't. I was living with the challenges and frustrations and heartbreaks that you now come to me with. Through the things I have shared here with you, I got from there to here, and you can, too.

I am the Messenger, and I live my life as an example of my message. I will ask no less of you. And, at the same time, I honor the process, yours and mine. I have had to learn to stop spraying a fire hose at people with my message or trying to drag them by the hair kicking and screaming across the finish line.

There are no failures, no mistakes. You are on your path, always, and this is your journey.

Everything that shows up is part of it. It all counts. It all matters.

We say, "What you think is in the way is the way." Another way to say this is, "The obstacle is the path."

Really get that.

As you grow and evolve right here right now, I am growing and evolving, too, into my What's Next. I continue to use all these teachings and tools in my own life as I share them with others. This book is a part of my What's Next. It's a pinnacle moment, a mountaintop experience.

I was asked when I was writing my first book and training to speak on stage and honing my message as a Transformational Coach, what keeps you up at night? What do you lose sleep over? What makes you crazy? That's an easy one! People living a life they don't love, working a soul-sucking job, struggling with money, experiencing pain in their relationships, unfulfilled, and all the while, frozen, stuck, paralyzed. These things make me want to rise up. I can't be quiet. Even more than that, I am crazy when I see people with so much to give the world not giving themselves the gift that matters the most. They come to me struggling with money and with illness and with relationship problems, and they are not showing up as who they are in the world and not doing what they are made to do.

I tell my clients, and I tell you that you have to make a decision like I did when I left a toxic marriage with a two-year-old, when I moved away to a new place and flung myself fully into the unknown and found the magic, when I left the career I thought I was building and went to graduate school as a mother of three kids under 7 to pursue a new career, when I left my job as a Therapist and gave up my license to make a big move and start my own business in a new place, again flinging myself fully into the unknown, when I answered the call into Seminary to become an ordained interfaith minister and hospital chaplain, and then again to complete my Doctorate in Transformational Spiritual Coaching based on the body of work I had created in my business, when I closed down my brick and mortar locations and moved my business online and global, when I wrote my first book, my second, my third, and now this one, my fourth, when I stepped on my first stage, when I shifted my business and brought my husband home into retirement and became a grandmother once and then twice, when I answered the call to live in a second location part of the year to serve at my highest and best as a teacher and leader, when I said yes to appearing on National TV to talk about this stuff and ended up with my own weekly segment, when I agreed to walk 100 miles of the Camino in Spain with my parents, my brother and sister and their spouses, and my husband and had all my stuff come up, and then I agreed to walk 100 miles in Italy on the Via Francigena, and then yet again to walk 100 miles in England this year on The Cotswold Way, and . . . whatever is next.

Everything I have is because of those moments.

By the way, if you ever want to work out all your stuff like I shared with you in this book, walk 100 miles with your family of origin. That is my next book.

With every yes, I shifted probabilities and possibilities, and moved things outside of my realm into my realm, creating my own future, one that I am happy to live with. At the same time, I had to learn to let go of what no longer served me.

I had to do three things to turn my life around. I had to Show Up, Make A Decision, and Take Aligned Action.

Be willing to stay in it for the long haul to get the results you want. Learn the Journey of Trust x3—Trust Yourself, Trust Divine Intelligence, and Trust the Process.

This book you are reading is part of the process you were led to. I am part of your process.

This is truly The Hero's Journey, and it's magnificent. One thing you can trust about me is that I always go first. This is what I teach, and this is how I live. I live my life, and I share my journey. I walk through fires, and then I turn around and help others get from where they are to where I am. I invest in myself both personally and professionally, I get the healing and the results, and then I teach what I have learned to others. I am committed to my own growth and evolution and the growth and evolution of my work in the world. I am committed to living my best life.

Come on, I know the way. I've been doing this a little while. I'll hold space for you, and I'll hold your hand.

I love working with people at this level, bringing all my gifts to the table to support and guide you through the inner work and the outer work.

So, here we are.
It's time.

M.O.V.E. or Be Moved. It's Always Your Choice.

Many of my clients share that they have this big thing they feel they are called to do in the world and to be in the world, both for themselves and for others. They feel a bigger life calling to them.

They want more fulfillment in their lives. They are experiencing exactly the longing that I knew for so many years before I began living a life of significance and success.

There was a time when I wasn't even sure what I wanted was possible. I was caught up in all my obligations and responsibilities and all the roles I was playing, and it didn't occur to me, yet, that I had created it. All of it. All the busyness in my life? I had created it myself. And then I used it as an excuse not to have what I wanted, be what I wanted, and do what I wanted.

What I want to share with you today is that it all starts with making a decision. Yep, you make a decision to create change. You DECIDE to move forward. Those first few steps in this direction can feel like wading in quicksand, but stay with it.

Imagine you are suddenly changing course and turning a huge ship or a giant jet plane. As you build momentum, you are uplifted into a new energy, and everything begins to move in your favor. The key is, you have to take the first step. Before everything shows up!

This is where a lot of my clients get tripped up. Because they are waiting. Waiting for better timing, more money, more security in a relationship, closure in a situation, and any number of things they perceive need attention. We're talking about your WHOLE life here, and all those things will get addressed once you start moving. In fact, a lot of it will begin to take care of itself in what feels like a very natural way. It will move with you.

It drives me crazy to see my clients and students and potential clients and students stuck HERE, in this place. Nothing happens here. Except that it eats away at you.

The best time is always NOW. You hear it. So why don't you believe it? What are you afraid of?

Now, What are YOU meant to BE, DO, and HAVE Next?

There are two aspects competing for your time, energy, and resources. One is life enhancing, and one if life depleting. One moves you toward what you want, and one moves you away from what you want. They are battling for it. Which one wins? Whichever one you feed.

Energy never stands still. You are ALWAYS either moving towards or away from what you desire. You make a decision, even with your indecision and inaction. You make a decision to put off your highest good, to turn a deaf ear or a blind eye to what is calling you to come forth. You are here for a purpose. You are a part of the plan. The life of your dreams, a life you love that supports you, is within reach. YOU have to create it. Every day. Consistently, boldly, relentlessly.

It all starts when you Make A Decision, the first step in my M.O.V.E. process for moving forward in any area of your life.

What decision can you make for your highest good today?

Know Yourself

Whenever you are thinking about making a big life transition, there are really three ways to go about it. Knowing yourself well can make a difference in the amount of stress you experience during this time as well as the amount of success you are able to create.

I talk a lot about taking honest inventory, and this is one of those times when the payoff for doing this consistently can be huge.

You want to pay attention both to the actions you are taking, and not taking, and to the energy you are carrying about it.

When working with clients who come to me ready to make a move or at least considering the possibility, I take some time with them first to explore their hardwiring and their mindset.

I have had clients who have successfully taken big leaps on the spot without much looking back at all and have been able to move forward very quickly without experiencing a lot of fallout. The energy they are holding is that as they go off the side of that cliff, either the road will rise up to meet them or they will grow wings and be taught how to fly. The key to making this work is that they immediately get into massive action and stay in massive action.

Know yourself. If you are not a risk-taker, the stress you may cause yourself in taking the big leap will work against the positive energy you need to "just keep swimming." For these clients, I suggest they determine what I call a tolerate date. They are using up valuable time and energy spinning in how much they don't like where they are and how unhappy they are, and they get into a lot of asking how things might change for them. By setting a date with yourself, the absolute maximum time you are willing to tolerate these circumstances, you stop the mind's endless chatter about it, and you satisfy its need to know.

Is it time for you to SET A TOLERATE DATE?

Now, everything will begin to conspire to work for you toward that goal, and you are no longer working against yourself. As you shift from the negative energy to the positive energy, you begin to be different and to do things differently, and things start to come together for your benefit. Very often, people end up coming out of their undesirable circumstances much sooner than the date they set, and it happens in a much more natural way.

Then there are those who continue to work with the positive energy of their growing desire. They are visualizing it, feeling it, and sending their order out to the Universe. But they are not taking any action, and they have not set any goals. What most often happens here is that as the desire grows stronger and the feelings associated with it become a part of who you are, the Universe begins to work in your favor in response to your ever-increasing desire. Because you are not taking action, you are not creating space, and you are not letting go of what no longer serves you. What you end up seeing here is the rug being ripped out from under you. This is when you are suddenly forced out of a job, a home, a relationship, or a geographical location.

Each of these is a choice. The more responsibility you are willing to take, the more power you are given over your own life. It is all about becoming conscious and aware and taking action.

What Is My Next Step?

You only need to know the next step to take the next step.

Too often, people come to me for coaching, for support and guidance, and they are just sitting and spinning in place because they don't know all the steps. And, so, they take no steps. I work with both ledge leapers and baby steppers, and it doesn't matter which one you are or what you are most comfortable doing right now, it's all about taking that next step. That is the only way the steps beyond that will show themselves to you.

ACT, ASSESS, ADJUST

Don't waste any more time sitting still. You are ready to get moving forward in the direction of your dreams and desires to create a better life now. Know that there are no mistakes, and you cannot fail. You have a tool, Course Correction, that you can use, as you are learning to read feedback from the Universe. Get into a quiet, reflective, or meditative state and ask yourself, that part of you that already knows the answers, "What is my next step?"

Remember, you only need to know the next step to take the next step.

Imagine if you are planning on driving from the West Coast to the East Coast. You have a map, so you know the direction you want to move in, and you have a destination where you would like to arrive. Even with a map, you cannot know and plan for everything that will show up along the way. You trust yourself to make this journey. You are prepared. You have made a decision to go, and you are committed.

Imagine that you are traveling at night. You can only see as far as your headlights shine out in front of you, and you make the journey this way all night long. You cannot, of course, see all the way from the West Coast to the East Coast, and every step you take, every mile you travel, everything is changing in every moment. People are coming and going and may or may not cross your path depending on the decisions and choices you make. You even have a choice of routes to take. You get to determine your speed and whether you want to get there fast or take a more scenic route, whether you want to stop along the way and visit people or places, learn things, or simply rest.

You would not question in the middle of this journey whether or not you will still end up at your destination? Will I be able to get to the East Coast? You would not doubt and turn back out of fear. You would keep moving forward. If you got stuck, you would get help. If you got lost, you would stop and get some better directions.

This journey is much the same.

As you move along, you are changing every minute, with every person and thing that crosses your path, and with every experience you have, all that you encounter. You are different halfway through the journey than you were at the beginning. You have seen different things, thought different things, learned different things, experienced different things, and felt different things, most likely even made some changes in your plans along the way. The longer the journey from here to there, the more this will happen for you.

Delight in the journey. There is so much to experience along the way. Here is a gift for you. Be excited for your journey. Your journey is now and always has been. You have never not been on your journey, on your path. No matter the U-turns, the distractions, the turning back, the side trips, and the stops you have made along the way, you are journeying.

The more you can enjoy the journey and being with yourself on this journey, supporting yourself unconditionally, the better it will be for you.

What is my next step? Ask yourself this.

Here's the important part of this, and every successful person will tell you this, when you receive that next step, you need to move into action. Take that next step. Because once you do, then the next one and the next one and the next one will unfold. Maybe you've heard the saying, "Remember, even if you're on the right track, you'll get run over if you just sit there."

I've been there. Hesitating, not moving, not taking action. Stuck in my stuff. So many of my clients come to me when they are exactly in this place. They get clarity, and they experience desire, then they keep getting in their own way and just sit there while everything around them is trying to come together to support them... if they would just move. That seems to be the place that gets people, that they have to take real-world physical third-dimensional action to manifest in this physical world what they want.

Sad to say, I have seen some of my clients and students, and I have experienced myself, the cosmic 2×4 come swinging around while I'm just sitting there. I call this a "brick-to-the-head" moment.

The best part of this is that you just need to take consistent baby steps in alignment with what you have told the Universe and yourself that you want. It's very effective, the baby steps. Just don't stop the momentum by standing still. Act, Assess, Adjust. Course correct.

Every day, ask yourself, "What is my next step?" Ask yourself, and ask your guidance, and when you get an answer, act on it. Do this every day. Do not miss a day. The more you work with this, the more quickly and frequently the answers will come.

Here's something to know about this, too. Do this every day. Often, you won't receive the answer right away while you are sitting there waiting for it. Sometimes you have to stop trying so hard, like when you're trying to remember a name so you can tell someone, and then suddenly you can't come up with it at all. So, do the asking, then go on with your business for the day. It will come in. Watch for it. Notice everything that shows up. Expect it. It will come in for you.

If you want to work on this consistently with daily support and guidance begin Day One of my 21-Day Email Course, my gift to you, to help you M.O.V.E. Forward in any area of your life at www.IntuitiveSuccessCoach.com. Experience what it's like to have your own personal success coach, and continue the journey we have begun here together. It's time to get moving in the direction of your dreams and desires and create a better life now! M.O.V.E. Forward in Any Area of Your Life in Just 21 Days with my Powerful Process! Give me just twenty minutes each day.

CHAPTER 19

Are You Merely Interested
or Committed?

*If you are interested, you will do what's convenient, but if you
are committed, you will do* **Whatever It Takes**.
—John Assaraf

I had the opportunity to spend some time with John Assaraf and to learn from him. This is by far the most powerful teaching he instilled in me that has stayed with me as a motivation and a measure. He asked, *"Are you interested or committed?"*

What a question, right? It makes you think, and it makes you take a stand for one side or the other. And, in order to answer his question, I had to stop playing with my expensive hobby. I had to stop dabbling and wobbling and wavering, allowing myself to make excuses, tell disempowering stories and be satisfied sitting on the edge, dipping my toes in the water and saying I was doing it. I was dreaming about all the things I could do and would do and how I could change my life so that it would be so much better.

The day came when I had to stop talking about not having it and have it!

He called me to action. It was another defining moment in my journey, another choice point.

I had to do three things to turn my life and my business around. I had to show up, make a decision, and take aligned action.

I had been bumping up against some of my own brick walls again, and I had to make yet another choice to either commit or retreat. I had learned that every choice I made and action I took moved me either toward or away from what I wanted. I also had learned that every single thing you think, feel, and do is either life depleting or life enhancing.

You are always either moving towards or away from what you need, want, and desire.. In each moment lies the opportunity to say, "I am doing this!," to face what is in your way, open up to the next step and move forward, and do what is necessary to create the future you deserve and desire.

I decided at a turning point in my life to not allow myself to wander in that desert anymore. I stopped ranting and raging and crying and throwing myself into the ditch. I was SO DONE with that. I rediscovered who I am, reconnected with what I am made to do and the life I wanted to live, and I committed, for real, to my greatness.

*I am here for a purpose and that purpose is to grow into a mountain, not to shrink to a grain of sand. Henceforth will I apply **All** my efforts to become the highest mountain of all and I will strain my potential until it cries for mercy.*
—Og Mandino

I no longer had reasons why I could not, would not, should not pursue my purpose. None of the reasons I had were good ones. I started making promises to myself that I would keep. I began to change from the inside out.

I shifted from resistance to receptivity. I opened to my own neverending growth and evolution.

The moment I committed to myself and to that greater something, everything changed. My whole life changed.

It is said that, "Until one is committed, there is hesitancy, the chance to draw back, always ineffectiveness. Concerning all acts of initiative (and creation), there is one elementary truth, the ignorance of which kills countless ideas and splendid plans: that the moment one definitely commits oneself, then Providence moves, too. All sorts of things occur to help one that would never otherwise have occurred. A whole stream of events issues from the decision, raising in one's favor all manner of unforeseen incidents and meetings and material assistance, which no man could have dreamed would have come his way." (J. W. von Goethe)

The magic happened, and it keeps happening!

I have learned that I always have to go first, and then the Universe will rush in to meet me. I have had a lot of clients come to me playing the when/then game. They give me a list of what they want and tell me they will do everything I recommend to them if I can guarantee they will get what they want from doing it. At the same time, they tell their Trusted Source, "When you provide me with all of this, then I will answer the call."

That's not how it works. We came here for the experience. A perfect plan does not pre-exist; it becomes as we grow and evolve. It's an organic process, and it's miraculous.

Do you want it badly enough?

I see a lot of desire out there, and it's escalating for many people. What stops people is the moment they need to commit to themselves to take specific consistent action.

I often find that the higher desire someone has for something that is really important to them, the higher resistance they encounter. This is the opportunity to dive in and create astounding transformation. And it's scary as hell getting started. What it always is, I am here to tell you, it is worth it. Beyond measure.

You have a future that you are meant to live, and it's been calling to you. Where there is desire, there is always the way. You are meant to be living this life now. So, what's holding you back?

I can look back now over all the years that I knew what I wanted and who I wanted to show up in the world as, and I didn't do anything about it. I had tons of excuses, and I created a lot of busyness and distraction in my world. I did a lot to numb those cravings for more, and I promised myself that someday—SOME DAY—I would make a move. Just not today, I'm not ready, I'm not prepared, just don't ask me to do anything about it today.

You will come to moments like these in your own life, facing the pain of staying the same and the fear of creating change, and every time you make a choice to either commit or retreat. You are always, ALWAYS, either moving towards or away from your goal, your vision, your mission, your truth and the life of your dreams. There is an energy to it. In every one of these moments lies the opportunity to say, "I am doing this!," to face what is in your way, open up to the next step and move forward, doing what is necessary to create the future you are meant to be living now.

Something very important is always hiding behind your resistance, behind your excuses and your fears and doubts, that keep you from making a commitment to yourself to step into who you are and take that out into the world. It's both the prison and the key to your freedom. Your choice in every moment defines it.

Right now is one of those moments. As you read this, something is being activated inside of you, and you have a choice.

If you are ready to truly change the way you show up in your life and in your work, ready to experience a new way of being in your career, in relationships, with money, if you find yourself in just this place, then I challenge you to make a renewed commitment to yourself and take action now, today. Do something, from taking the tiniest baby step to the greatest leap, to get moving towards all that you want.

You are meant to be living this life now.

Know this: "The moment you commit and quit holding back, all sorts of unforeseen incidents, meetings, and material assistance will rise up to help you. The simple act of commitment is a powerful magnet for help." (Napoleon Hill)

A Note about Risk-Taking

You may be really ready for a risk even after never having taken them; it can be such a liberating experience that yields magical results. I have been there and done it at a time when I disliked change and was very averse to risk-taking. My life since then has been absolutely worth it, my journey exciting and yielding out-of-this world results. It takes a "new" mindset and tremendous support. It takes preparation the way you would prepare for any journey. When the timing is right, you will feel it and know it. When nothing will stop you and you know you can't not do this thing, then you are ready. That is the exact time to take the big risks and let the Universe rush in to support you.

Thank You

I have loved sharing this journey with you, and if you'd like to continue on, I have a gift waiting for you, the Loving What's Next Masterclass that goes along with this book. Listen online or download it to go. Hear me as I teach you from this book, and experience a powerful process I will lead you through. In this class, I share with you some of the tools and processes I use when working with my clients individually and in Mastermind groups and programs.

You can claim your gift and gain immediate access at www.lovingwhatsnextgift.com.

About the Author

D r. Michelle Barr is a transformational coach and mindset mentor, helping you create and live your vision and find the freedom you desire and deserve. Michelle works with her clients and students intuitively, energetically, and strategically to gain clarity and take inspired action while clearing, healing, and resolving what is getting in the way.

Michelle has been a Personal Transformation Specialist for over thirty years. She holds a Master's Degree in Counseling and Guidance, an ordination and Seminary degree as an interfaith minister and hospital chaplain, and a Doctorate in Transformational Spiritual Coaching.

Michelle is a speaker, teacher, and author, and this is her fourth book.

Michelle lives in Texas with her husband of thirty-two years and travels from her home base all over the world speaking and teaching and serving.

Connect with Michelle on her website at www.michellebarr.com, where she has free gifts and resources waiting for you.

Connect with Michelle on Facebook at www.facebook.com/michellebbarr where she shows up every day to talk about these things and to teach, train, motivate, and inspire.

If you desire to be fed every day as you grow and evolve and transform, you can buy her 365-Day Book or Book and Journal, *#SoulTeach: Your Guide to Manifesting What You Need, Want, and Desire* at www.SoulTeachBook.com.

Listen to Michelle's powerful teachings and trainings on her Loving What's Next podcast at www.lovingwhatsnextpodcast.com.

A free ebook edition is available with the purchase of this book.

To claim your free ebook edition:
1. Visit MorganJamesBOGO.com
2. Sign your name CLEARLY in the space
3. Complete the form and submit a photo of the entire copyright page
4. You or your friend can download the ebook to your preferred device

Morgan James BOGO™

A **FREE** ebook edition is available for you or a friend with the purchase of this print book.

CLEARLY SIGN YOUR NAME ABOVE

Instructions to claim your free ebook edition:
1. Visit MorganJamesBOGO.com
2. Sign your name CLEARLY in the space above
3. Complete the form and submit a photo of this entire page
4. You or your friend can download the ebook to your preferred device

Print & Digital Together Forever.

Snap a photo   Free ebook   Read anywhere

www.ingramcontent.com/pod-product-compliance
Lightning Source LLC
Jackson TN
JSHW081500070125
76711JS00004B/54